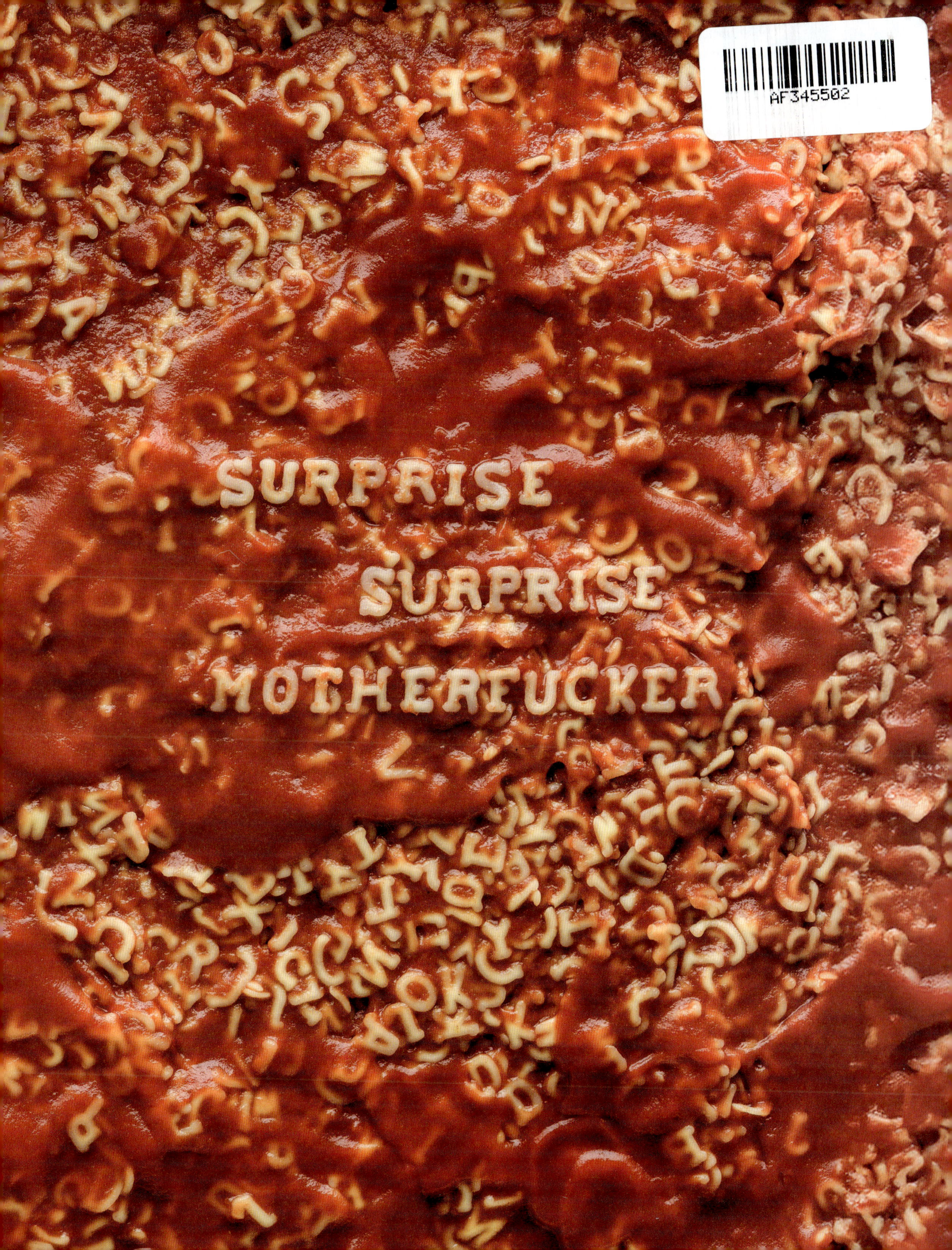

SURPRISE
SURPRISE
MOTHERFUCKER

Dedication

A Bianca e Flavio

Handmade pasta that makes chefs swear and nonnas proud.

AL DENTE AS F*CK

Lannoo

café coado

CONTENTS

YOU'LL NEVER LOOK AT STORE-BOUGHT PASTA

THE SAME WAY AGAIN

*Al Dente As F*ck*

YOU'LL NEVER LOOK AT STORE-BOUGHT PASTA THE SAME WAY AGAIN

Alright, listen up. Pasta is tradition, sure. It's passed down, it's sacred, it's the backbone of every nonna's kitchen. But let's be real: pasta is also the easiest, most accessible comfort food on the planet. Everyone has a pack of pasta sitting in their cupboard. It's fast, it's there for you, and it never disappoints. But here's the thing. Knowing how to *make* pasta? That's the real flex.

Don't get it twisted, this isn't nuclear physics. No lab coat required. You need exactly two things: 100 grams of flour and one egg. No magic tricks, no heavy machinery, no secret ingredients. Just you, your hands, and a little patience. Despite what you've heard, pasta is also *forgiving*. It's not some diva ingredient that throws a tantrum if you don't nail it on the first try. If it's too dry? Add more egg. Too sticky? More flour. Relax. Take a breath. Knead the damn dough and you'll be fine.

Unlike ripping open a packet, this takes a little effort – it's hands-on, it's messy, and it's something you only get good at by doing it a lot. So don't start by making a mountain of it. Go small. Practice. Get a feel for it. Then, when you're ready? You'll never look at store-bought pasta the same way again. Look, we're not here to shame anyone for buying dried pasta at the supermarket. We get it. It's convenient and it's cheap. It cooks in under ten minutes and sometimes that's all your weeknight can handle. But once you've made your own pasta, once you've felt that dough go from shaggy mess to silky smooth, once you've rolled it thin enough to read your ex's texts through it, something shifts. Before you know it, you'll start saying things like "This tagliatelle has too much bite" and "I prefer my ravioli with a lower hydration dough." You'll start judging restaurants not by the wine list, but by the width of their pappardelle.

When it comes to pasta, we believe in chaos, not compartments. There is no single Italian nonna whispering in our ears. There are twelve. They're all yelling. One says "Put more egg!" Another says "You rolled it too thick!" One just mutters *"Che vergogna…"* as she watches you stuff your tortellini like a burrito. We respect all nonnas – as should you – but we believe that pasta doesn't have to be married to tradition. You can mix your heritage with your leftovers, and shove it all into a raviolo. That's not disrespectful in our book. That's evolution, baby. In this book you'll find kimchi and miso, but also a ragù so historic it should be in a museum. There are sauces that don't get cooked and shapes that don't have names.

It could well be that your first batch of handmade pasta won't look like a pasta influencer's victory reel. Maybe your dough tears. Maybe your farfalle look like roadkill. Doesn't matter. You'll get the hang of it. And when someone you serve a bowl of handmade pasta to takes a bite and says "Wait, you made this from scratch?" you'll grin, shrug, and feel a sense of pride that's unlike anything else.

Pasta pride.

HOW TWO CHEFS GOT STUCK INDOORS AND

DECIDED TO CHANGE THE PASTA GAME

HOW TWO CHEFS GOT STUCK INDOORS AND DECIDED TO CHANGE THE PASTA GAME

Pastology was born during the second lockdown. Picture it: two Italian chefs, too much time on their hands, and an almost illegal amount of flour. What do you do? You make pasta. Lots of it. What started as a way to stay busy (and avoid losing our minds) quickly turned into something bigger. We started feeding friends, then friends of friends, then actual customers willing to pay for the privilege of eating fresh pasta made by two slightly unhinged Italians. Turns out, people really like good pasta — who'd have thought?

Bruna: The Big Mouth with a Big Passion

Bruna didn't start her career in a kitchen – far from it. First she studied law, and following that, veterinary medicine. Then she trained young horses. Then she worked as a volunteer with big cats. In short, she had absolutely zero professional training as a chef. But life has a way of throwing you into the fire when you least expect it. She needed money, fast, to support her horses, so she knocked on the door of the Alajmo family, the owners of Le Calandre, a 3-Michelin-star restaurant she had been going to with her parents in Rubano – and asked for a job. They put her in front of house, and from there, one thing led to another.

At some point, she had to face the truth: she didn't want to be a lawyer, a horse trainer, or a wildlife rescuer. She was going through her nonna's old recipe books and something clicked. She wanted to cook. Telling her mother was like a coming out moment, except instead of a dramatic confession, it went like this: "I don't want to study anymore. I want to be a chef. And I need to go to culinary school."

But before she could even think about school, she had to get into a kitchen. And here's the fun part: when she asked for a stage in the kitchen at Le Calandre, Alajmo himself basically said, "No way. You're the fun one in front of house. Too loud. Too opinionated. Less than zero experience." So off she went to Belle Parti in Padova instead, where she finally got her hands on the real work of a kitchen. Needless to say, it was a very humbling experience.

From there, she built her career with the same mix of raw passion, stubbornness, and an endless stream of curse words that still define her today. Bruna doesn't just cook, she takes over the kitchen. Loud, impulsive, and with a vocabulary that could make a sailor blush, she's the kind of person who turns food into an event.

Emanuele: The Nitpick Ninja

Emanuele, unlike Bruna, was never chaos. He was order, detail, the steady hand that straightens a knife on the pass when no one is looking. Born in Rome, raised in restaurants, he grew up convinced of one thing: food wasn't a job, it was destiny.

At eighteen he left home with little more than ambition and a friend at his side. London swallowed him whole, and Novikov in Mayfair became his battlefield, an Italian restaurant so busy that survival meant moving faster than lightning. But France called, and Lyon gave him something different: not just training in a Michelin-star kitchen, Tetedoie*, but a whole new culture of food and hospitality, a way of living and breathing gastronomy that was unlike anything he had known before.

London pulled him back again, this time by way of Restaurant Gordon Ramsay***. Under Clare Smyth and Matt Abé he discovered the other side of cooking at the very top: discipline, precision, and setting the highest possible standard, day after day.

Italy then brought him home, and with Lele Usai at Il Tino* he reconnected with the essence of pasta. Flour and eggs became more than ingredients; they were geometry, memory, identity. Pasta was no longer "a dish", it was who he was becoming.

Then came Zeeland. At Pure C**, working for Sergio Herman, he met Bruna, earned a second Michelin star, and began to understand the place that would one day become home. Later, with Filip Claeys at De Jonkman** in Bruges, he discovered a deeper responsibility: cooking with the sea, treating fish not just as produce, but as a living resource to be respected and sustained.

All of it: London's fire, France's culture, Italy's soul, Zeeland's sea shaped him. And eventually, the kitchens of others were no longer enough. The time had come to build his own. That's when Pastology was born.

Mediocrity? Not in his vocabulary. Every millimeter of dough, every second of cooking time, every gram of flour, he notices everything. He's methodical, technical, and just a tiny bit of a pain in the ass when it comes to details. If Bruna is the impulse buy, Emanuele is the return policy.

Today, every bite of Pastology's pasta carries the weight of his obsession; perfection, or nothing.

*Al Dente As F*ck*

We met in the kitchen of Pure C, a restaurant in Cadzand Bad, a picturesque village in Zeeland in the Netherlands. If you don't know where that is, don't worry, neither did we until we got there. From the kitchen windows we could see peaceful Zeeland and the grey North Sea. But inside it was absolute madness: crazy complicated preparations and hardly any time to execute them, loads of "Behind!" being shouted, and loud (very loud) techno music. We instantly felt at home.

It wasn't love at first sight. In fact, it was more like "Who the hell is this person, and why do they speak Italian so wrong?" Bruna's fast-talking Padova accent and Emanuele's Roman precision clashed like two angry nonni arguing over the right way to make carbonara. But when we cooked together, it *worked*. Sure, we fought. We fought over recipes, techniques, and who was leaving the pasta out to dry for too long. But in the kitchen, our differences made us better.

Following our gut is maybe the only thing we have in common. We fell in love, had two kids, and started a business. When life throws you into the middle of nowhere with a rolling pin and a bag of flour, you either lose your mind or start a pasta movement. We chose the second option. Side note: we didn't start Pastology thinking "Let's build a pasta empire." We started it thinking "What if we just made really, really good pasta and didn't completely kill each other in the process?"

In the beginning, we worked out of the tiniest kitchen imaginable. Zero staff, zero budget, and a lot of shouting. Romantic? Only if your idea of romance involves flour in your ears and someone crying over a broken raviolo at midnight. We said yes to everything: private dinners, subscription boxes, wholesale deals with restaurants who didn't pay us until months after the fact. The full start-up starter pack. We worked like maniacs.

And then people started paying attention. Someone sent us a message that read "I haven't tasted pasta like this since I was in Bologna." We kept going. When making pasta at home was no longer cute chaos, we moved production into a real workspace. A shiny new atelier. Turns out, what we thought was a big step forward was just a temporary lull in the madness. The space filled up instantly. Fridges, tables, trays of pasta stacked to the ceiling, flour in every corner. We're right back to where we started, just with more bills and better lighting.

This book is not a tribute to tradition, it's a love letter to chaos, carbs, and shouting across the kitchen table. If you're here, it means you believe in pasta with a generous side of personality.

Welcome to Pastology.

How two chefs got stuck indoors and decided to change the pasta game

A BRIEF — AND BRUTALLY HONEST — HISTORY OF PASTA

A BRIEF — AND BRUTALLY HONEST — HISTORY OF PASTA

Let's clear the table: Marco Polo did not bring pasta to Italy from China. That myth is older than your nonna's moka pot and twice as wrong. Pasta was already a thing in the Mediterranean way before Polo packed his tiny explorer bag. We're talking ancient civilizations already turning wheat into dough while he was still twinkling in his papa's eye.

The Ancient Carbohydrate Timeline (Real Edition)

~400 BCE – The Greeks and the word "laganon"

They used this term for a flat dough cut into strips. Ding ding! Early lasagna, baby. No layers, no béchamel, but the vibe was there.

~1000 BCE – The Etruscans

These pre-Roman badasses were already making proto-pasta from ground grains and water. No eggs, no machines – just mortars, stones, and attitude. They flattened the dough into sheets and cooked it. Sound familiar?

~1st century CE – The Romans (aka Carbo Supreme)

Romans were OBSESSED with flour and water. They didn't call it "pasta," but they boiled sheets (*laganum*), baked layered dishes, and even stuffed dough. Apicius (think: Roman Gordon Ramsay) wrote recipes that wouldn't look out of place on your Sunday table.

9th–11th centuries CE – Arab influence in Sicily

Here's the big plot twist: it was likely the Arabs – settled in Sicily – who introduced the concept of dried pasta (*itriyya*) made from durum wheat semolina. Why? Because they needed food that could survive the journey across deserts and seas. The Arabs brought the *science*; southern Italians brought the *sauce*.

14th-17th centuries CE – Egg Pasta Enters the Chat

Egg pasta comes later and it's all about the north. In the Renaissance, richer regions like Emilia-Romagna started adding eggs to soft wheat flour. The result? Silky dough, thinner sheets, and a new standard of bougie deliciousness. This wasn't poor people food anymore. These were *noble carbs*. You needed chickens. You needed time. You needed *skill*. That's when filled pasta exploded – tortellini, cappelletti, agnolotti – all designed to cradle a perfect bite like a little carbohydrate cradle of love.

By the 1200s – Pasta goes commercial

Palermo, Sicily was already poppin' with pasta production. Historical records talk about factories exporting dried noodles across the Mediterranean. Not romantic nonnas on balconies – *factories*. By the 13th century, the city of Genoa was full-on trading dried pasta. Why? Shelf life. Easy transport. Deliciousness. Pasta became the canned beans of the Middle Ages, but way tastier.

Pasta Today: From Sacred to Screwed (Sometimes)

Fast forward to now. Pasta is global. Industrial. Ubiquitous. You can buy it at the gas station, eat it in space, or watch it get disrespected in 30 million YouTube videos. But none of that makes it any less iconic. Because when done right – when *made* right – it still hits like the first time. It still carries the weight of centuries. Of migration, poverty, innovation, love, and stubborn Italian grandmas who could cut tagliatelle by eye better than your kitchen scale ever will.

*Al Dente As F*ck*

Pasta Shapes, Regional Sass (And Why Every Town Thinks They Invented It All)

Let's get one thing straight: in Italy, pasta is local as hell. We're not talking north versus south. We're talking village versus village, nonna versus nonna, "that one house on the hill" versus literally everyone else. Every place swears that their pasta is the original, the best, the purest form of carb expression. And you know what? They're not totally wrong. Because pasta didn't come from one lab, one kitchen, or one single recipe. It *evolved*. It adapted. It grew roots in the flour of each region, shaped by climate, culture, and whatever the hell was in the pantry at the time.

Each shape tells you something about local traditions, local ingredients, and cultural expression. Sardinia? They roll maloreddus like their lives depend on it and sometimes it does, depending on the dinner guest. Emilia-Romagna? They fold tortellini so tight you'd think they were wrapping national secrets.

In Liguria, they make trofie that twist like gossip. And in Puglia? Orecchiette, also known as 'little ears', because who doesn't like to think of severed body parts when eating a bowl of pasta.

From long strands to short cuts and intricate hand-shaped pasta pieces, every shape is designed with a purpose – to envelop hearty fillings, to delicately float in broth or to layer in between rich sauces. And let's not forget that *every* town insists they were the first to invent a specific shape. And they will absolutely fight you over it. Not physically, but definitely with long-winded monologues, fifteen competing stories, and one surviving great-aunt who "remembers how it was really done." Honestly? We love the drama.

That's what makes pasta so magical. It isn't a static ingredient, but a shapeshifter. It's a peasant dish turned into an art form, a daily staple that has become a true cultural identity. One village dries its pasta on straw, another rolls it over knitting needles, and someone's great-grandpa used to shape it around his pinky finger while smoking a cigar.

No matter how many shapes you think you know, there's always more. Pasta historians (yes, that's a thing) keep discovering or reviving obscure forms, like endangered species in the wild. Some look like flowers, some like shells, some like something you probably shouldn't say out loud. They're the edible history of Italy.

Let's Go on a Quick Road Trip

To Italians, shape matters. Texture matters. Origin really f*cking matters. Italy isn't just a country; it's a complicated pasta map steeped in hyper-local pride. Every region has its signature shape, and woe unto you if you mix them up. Let's hit the carb road, from north to south.

Piemonte

In Piemonte, pasta takes the form of *tajarin*. Delicate golden ribbons cut as fine as silk. What makes them remarkable is the dough, enriched with an almost scandalous number of egg yolks, giving the pasta a deep color and an indulgent flavor. Traditionally paired with butter, sage, or shaved truffle.

Liguria

In Italy's coastal armpit, we find *trofie*, small hand-rolled twists that look as though the pasta dough has tried to braid itself. Their shape is no accident: the grooves and spirals are perfectly designed to hold pesto Genovese, which is basically a religion here.

Veneto

Bigoli are at home in Veneto. They're thick strands, traditionally extruded through a bronze die, and often made with duck eggs or even anchovy water if you're hardcore. They've got bite, and they've got a salty attitude. Just like the Veneti people.

Emilia-Romagna

The show-off region, Emilia-Romagna boasts a repertoire that borders on legendary: *tagliatelle, tortellini, cappelletti, lasagne*. Never utter the words "spaghetti Bolognese" here. Their ragù goes with tagliatelle and tagliatelle only.

Tuscany

Tuscany brings thick *pici* to the table. Rolled by hand, one lonely strand at a time. No eggs, no fancy gear, made simply from flour and water and some stubborn wrist action. They're uneven and chewy, drinking up sauce like a camel at an oasis.

Puglia

In the sun-soaked south, *orecchiette* reign supreme. Meaning "little ears," they're shaped with your thumb, no tools allowed (don't tell anyone we let you use a butter knife in our recipe). The edges are thicker than the center, which means they catch sauce like champs. Especially good with broccoli rabe and anchovies.

Sardinia

Off the mainland, Sardinia has its own distinctive pasta: *malloreddus*, also called gnocchetti sardi. Small semolina ridged nuggets, made by rolling bits of dough over a gnocchi board or wicker basket. They might look simple, but outside of Sardinia no one ever gets them just right. Island rules apply.

*Al Dente As F*ck*

A brief – and brutally honest – history of pasta

Ask someone from Bari how to make orecchiette and they'll say: *"Come te lo devo spiegare? Le mani."* (This loosely translates to: "How can I explain this to you, you dumbass? With your hands.") There's no one recipe. No clear step-by-step guide. No QR code. Just generations of muscle memory, thumb presses, and women sitting around a table saying *"così, guarda"* ("like this, look"). Ask someone from Rome why their carbonara is superior and they'll just blink at you like they don't understand the question.

Recipes aren't just passed down, they're inherited. When you grow up Italian, no one teaches you how to cook. You just stand around the kitchen, absorbing a thousand tiny rules by watching your family at work. How to salt water. When to flip the raviolo. What kind of pasta shape goes with what kind of sauce. And the further you get away from Italy, the louder those rules get. The more a dish travels, the more people cling to *their* version of it. Italian-Americans, for example, will fight you over sauce, they want plenty of it. Northern Italians will fight you over butter versus oil. Sicilians will fight you over everything.

Pasta holds memory, geography, family history and the joy of eating all in one plate. But it can also be science: flour ratios, hydration, egg weight, protein content. And it's geometry, when you're folding cappelletti or pinching tortellini or cutting tagliatelle just so. It's anthropology, in how every region, every village, every family created shapes and sauces to fit their land and their people. And it's magic, in the way a few humble ingredients can become comfort, elegance, tradition, rebellion.

Whether you're rolling tagliatelle in a Michelin-star kitchen, shaping gnocchi on your nonna's table, or squishing orecchiette while a baby screams and flour gets in your hair, you're doing something ancient. Something beautiful. Something that ties you to a long, delicious lineage. Don't be intimidated by tradition. Get your hands dirty. Get flour in your nails. Fight with your partner about the shape. Burn the first batch. Forget to salt the water. It's fine. Pasta isn't about being perfect, it's about being present. You're not just following a recipe. You're becoming part of a story.

A story told in ridges and folds, in egg yolks and rolling pins, in dried semola dust and sauce-stained shirts. A story of how we eat, how we love, how we remember, how we gather. A story that starts with flour, and ends with someone saying "Shut up and eat, it's getting cold."

So learn it. Own it. Twist it. Boil it. Shape it. Respect it. And above all, don't overcook it. Ever. Never ever. It needs to be al dente as f*ck.

WHY MAKING PASTA BY HAND IS A POWER MOVE

IS A POWER MOVE

AND HOW TO NOT SUCK AT IT

WHY MAKING PASTA BY HAND IS A POWER MOVE AND HOW TO NOT SUCK AT IT

Here's the deal: making your own pasta is badass. Not because it's trendy. Not because it's 'authentic'. But because it means taking back control. You're not relying on some anonymous factory in Parma. You're not boiling corporate spaghetti. You're literally putting your hands in flour and saying, "I got this." And the best part? Pasta doesn't gatekeep. It doesn't care if you've trained at Le Cordon Bleu or if you just binge-watched three episodes of Stanley Tucci: Searching For Italy. *What pasta cares about is attention, respect, and a decent level of humidity.*

Pasta Is Forgiving… Until It Isn't

Let's kill the myth: pasta dough isn't hard. What it is: responsive. It reacts to your touch. Too sticky? Add flour. Too dry? Add a few drops of water or a bit more egg. Knead like you mean it. Let it take a nap. Don't rush. Don't panic. Just vibe with it.

Making pasta is not an act of perfection, it's an act of presence. But yeah, if you mess up the ratio or treat the dough like it's Play-Doh, you'll know. Pasta doesn't lie.

A Ritual that Grounds You

In a world of 3-minute noodles and 15-second TikToks, making pasta from scratch is a full-on rebellion. It slows you down. It requires focus. It connects you to a rhythm older than your last ten ancestors combined. People meditate. People journal. You? You knead dough. And the result? Something infinitely more satisfying than therapy. (And much cheaper.)

You can't doomscroll while your hands are covered in flour. You can't answer emails mid-fold. And for once, your brain doesn't bounce between 12 tabs. You count eggs. You roll sheets. You breathe. Not to be mindful, but because if you zone out, you'll rip the dough and swear loudly enough to scare the dog. It's about doing one thing, just *one*, really, really well. And when was the last time you let yourself do that?

Let's Calm the Hell Down

Listen, if the whole "volcano of flour on the counter" thing gives you anxiety – breathe. You don't have to go full rustic warrior on your first try. Grab a big mixing bowl and make the dough in there. It keeps things clean, controlled, and non-traumatic.

Once you get the feel for it (and stop flinching every time an egg moves), then you can graduate to countertop chaos. Nobody's judging. The flour doesn't know where it is. Everyone's first pasta dough is a hot mess. It might be shaggy, sticky, or somehow both. Doesn't matter. It's not about aesthetics, and you learn by doing.

Don't Start with Lasagna Sheets

If this is your first pasta rodeo, calm down, cowboy. Start small. Try tagliatelle: easy to roll, easy to cut, hard to fuck up. Avoid filled pasta at first. Ravioli is a diva. Tortellini? Pure drama. Come back to those once you've learned to tame the dough, like a carb-whisperer.

Once your hands know what they're doing, the rest will follow. Muscle memory is real, and pasta respects hustle.

Hands Over Machines (at Least at First)

Could you use a stand mixer? Yes. Could you buy an electric extruder, cry yourself to sleep, and call it a day? Also yes. But if you want to understand pasta, you first need to make it the way your ancestors did: with your own damn hands.

Feel the dough change under your palms. Notice how it resists, then yields. That's gluten development. That's structure. That's chemistry *and* poetry. Once you've done it by hand a few times, then bring in the gadgets. Until then: no shortcuts. This is your Rocky montage.

Yes, You Can Use a Stand Mixer (But Don't Be a Hero)

Want to use your stand mixer or whatever shiny dough hook contraption you got for Christmas? Fine. Go for it. But – and this is a big BUT – go slow. Like, *slower than your last situationship* slow. Start on the lowest setting and watch that thing like you're a detective on a stakeout. If you blast it on level 6, you'll either burn out the motor or launch a flour bomb across your kitchen.

The mixer is a tool, not a babysitter. If it starts smoking or making noises like it's possessed? That's on you.

So, you're ready to make your first dough? Amazing. But before you go full *"nonna-core"*, here's what you actually need and what you absolutely don't.

WHAT YOU NEED:

1. Flour (and not just any flour)
This is your base. Your canvas. Your foundation. Choose right.

For egg pasta:
Get "00" flour (*doppio zero*). It's finely milled wheat flour, low in protein, and perfect for silky sheets. No "00" around? Use all-purpose, but sift it. Twice. Don't argue.

For semolina dough:
Look for *semola rimacinata di grano duro* – coarse re-milled durum wheat semolina. It should be rough, golden, and slightly gritty. If it looks like beach sand, you're on the right track.

2. Eggs (but fresh ones, yeah?)
Room temperature, preferably organic or from chickens that live a decent life. Red or bright orange yolks, folks. If your eggs are sad and pale, your pasta will be too.

3. Water (for real, don't overthink it)
Tap water is fine. Cold or lukewarm. If your city has sketchy water, use filtered. But seriously, this isn't *Breaking Bad*.

4. A flat surface
Wood is king. Marble works. A big-ass cutting board if you're broke. Just make sure it's clean, dry, and yours.

5. A rolling pin or a bottle of wine
Yes, a bottle of wine works in a pinch. Just don't drink it *before* you're done rolling, genius.

6. A knife, a fork, and your hands
You don't need anything fancy to start. The pasta machine can wait. Your fingers are your best tools.

WHAT YOU DON'T NEED (YET):

- *All* the pasta attachments for your superdeluxe stand mixer. You're not opening a trattoria. Chill.

- A drying rack, unless you're making kilos of pasta. A clean broomstick or the back of a chair will do the job. Or hang it on your arm and feel like Michelangelo's Vitruvian Man..

- Fancy imported flour from a monastery in the Alps. Cute, but unnecessary. Know your basics first.

- Your friend Marco who "did a course in Bologna once". He'll just confuse you and say 'al dente' too often.

This is pasta. Not a moon landing. Don't overthink it. Get the right ingredients, clear your schedule, and *go feel the dough*.

THE HOLY TRINITY

OF PASTA
MOTHER DOUGHS

THE HOLY TRINITY OF PASTA MOTHER DOUGHS

Let's start with the basics. Pasta isn't just food; it's an ancient form of edible engineering, passed down through generations with the same reverence people reserve for sacred texts or vintage red Ferraris. But before we get into shapes, recipes, and sauces, let's talk about what pasta actually is. There are three foundational doughs. Three big boys. The Holy Trinity. And yes, they all slap — but differently.

Dough #1: The No-nonsense No Egg Dough.

This is the OG. A mix of flour and water, nothing more. But plot twist: it actually has a split personality, this dough. You can make it with *semola* (for a bit more chew), or with *00 flour* (for softer, silky folds and more northern elegance). Same hydration level, different soul. We didn't want to separate them, so we didn't. You get both recipes. Because we're generous like that.

Dough #2: The Classic Egg Dough.

This is your standard nonna-style *pasta all'uovo*: 00 flour + whole eggs. Reliable and friendly. Great for everything from tagliatelle to lasagna sheets to ravioli. This dough is the eldest sibling: responsible, well-behaved, slightly overachieving.

Dough 3: The Power Dough.

This one is yolk porn. Rich, luxurious, dramatic. All 00 flour, just the single egg white and yolks on yolks on yolks. It's high-maintenance, sure, but it's worth it. Think pasta that holds its shape, has that gorgeous deep yellow color, and cooks like it's been to finishing school. It's your tortellini and cappelletti MVP. Fancy but not fragile.

So… why are there four recipes in this chapter if the doughs are three? Good question. Gold star for paying attention. The answer? Because we like chaos. And because you need options. See, one of the doughs (the eggless one) is a Gemini. It can be made with semola for those gritty, grip-it-good southern shapes, or with 00 flour for soft folds and silky moves. Same ratios, different moods. Do you need both in your life? Yes. Will you probably pick a favourite and pretend the other doesn't exist? Also yes.

Three doughs, four recipes, infinite possibilities. We know you probably came here for the sexy sauces and dramatic fillings, but trust us when we say: your pasta is only as good as your dough. First you need to get the basics right. Once you know your dough, you can go anywhere. You want pici? You got it. You want angel-hair-fine tagliolini? Let's roll.

Take your time. Read the dough recipes thoroughly. Get your hands in there. The rest of the book will wait for you. (But your dough won't so don't overhydrate it.)

1. Semola & Water Pasta –
Southern Grit, No Frills

Ingredients: Durum wheat semola + water. That's it. That's the tweet.

This is the tough, sunbaked dough of the south: Puglia, Basilicata, Calabria, Sicily, Campania. It's the pasta of resilience, made in regions where eggs were a luxury and semola reigned supreme. If egg pasta is a violin, semola pasta is a drumline: bold, rhythmic, and ready to carry any sauce with backbone.

Semola (from the Latin *simila*, meaning flour) is a coarse, golden grind of hard durum wheat. High in protein, low in bullshit. When hydrated and kneaded, it creates a firm, elastic dough that holds up beautifully under pressure. Its sister, semolina or *semola rimacinata* is perfect for extruded shapes like penne, rigatoni, maccheroni, fusilli, and orecchiette.

Also: semolina dough is what you'll find in industrial dried pasta today. Not because it's cheap but because it's strong, shelf-stable, and tastes like home.

Ingredients (Precise AF Edition, per 2 people):
- 200 g durum wheat semola flour
- 90–100 g lukewarm water
- A pinch of salt

Step 1: Mount Carbohydrate
Dump your 200 g of semola onto a clean surface like you're starting a ritual. Make a little well in the center. This is not for aesthetics – it's for control.

Step 2: Water In, Slowly
Start with 90 g of lukewarm water. Pour it little by little into the well, mixing with a fork or your fingers. If it's too dry, go up to 100 g max. No more. Don't be that guy.

Step 3: Knead Like You're Mad at It
Once it starts sticking together, go full hands-on. Knead for 10 minutes. It'll feel stiff and stubborn, like an old man yelling at clouds. That means it's working.

Step 4: Let It Chill
Form the dough into a ball, wrap it in plastic wrap or a damp towel, and let it rest for at least 30 minutes. This isn't a suggestion. This is where the magic happens.

Step 5: Shape That Baby
Cut off chunks and shape them however you want: orecchiette, trofie, cavatelli, malloreddus. No molds. No machines. Just you and your thumbs.

Step 6: Boil & Bite
Cook in heavily salted water (like, sea-level salty). Fresh semolina pasta takes 2–4 minutes, depending on thickness. Taste it. If it bites back, it's ready.

2. "00" & Water Pasta –
The Underdog with Big Vibes

Ingredients: Soft wheat flour ("00" or all-purpose) + water.

No eggs, no semolina. Just simplicity and your hands. This dough is historically common in central Italy, especially in Tuscany and Umbria, but it shows up in various hand-shaped forms all over the peninsula. Think pici, strangozzi, cavatelli (shared custody with semola in the south), trofie.

It's soft, malleable, forgiving. Great for beginners, great for artists. It doesn't need a machine or a press. Just a board, a knife, and maybe your thumb. It's the acoustic rock of pasta doughs. Minimalist, raw, powerful. Less showy than its cousins, but no less legit.

Ingredients (Soft but Strong, per 2 people):
- 200 g "00" flour (or all-purpose if you're desperate, but sift it like your reputation depends on it)
- 90–100 g lukewarm water
- A pinch of salt (optional, but makes you look like you know what you're doing)

Step 1: Flour Bomb Incoming
Pour 200 g of "00" flour onto your surface like you're opening a bakery in your kitchen. Make that little volcano in the center. You know the drill.

Step 2: Gently Hydrate
Add 90 g of lukewarm water slowly, mixing as you go. If it's too dry, bump it up to 100 g – *but don't just dump it in all at once like a maniac.*

Step 3: Knead to Believe
Knead that dough like it owes you money. You want it smooth, elastic, and just slightly tacky, like a good pop song. Give it a good 8–10 minutes of love. No shortcuts. You're not making Play-Doh.

Step 4: Let It Nap
Wrap it in plastic or a damp cloth and let it rest for 30 minutes. Gluten needs to chill so you can roll without tears (yours, not the dough's).

Step 5: Shape It Your Way
This dough is soft, obedient, and perfect for hand-shaped pasta:
- Roll it into snakes for pici
- Slice into strips for strangozzi
- Twist it for trofie
- Pinch it into cavatelli

No eggs = no stress. Just flour, water, and ancestral vibes.

Step 6: Cook It With Respect
Boil in salty water (like, "Adriatic levels" salty). Cooking time: 2–4 minutes, depending on how thick your shapes are. Taste it. Trust your teeth.

The holy trinity of pasta mother doughs

3. Egg Pasta –
Northern Elegance with Chicken Privilege

Ingredients: Soft wheat flour (ideally "00") + fresh eggs. That's it. Two ingredients, infinite possibilities, zero excuses.

This dough is smooth, tender, and rich – like the heir to an agriturismo fortune. It rolls out like silk and cooks fast. You'll find it in tagliatelle, pappardelle, fettuccine, ravioli, tortellini, basically any pasta that needs to be thin, pliable, and smooth enough to seduce a ragù.

Egg pasta is the queen of central and northern Italy, especially Emilia-Romagna, where they treat it like religion. And rightfully so. This region is home to Bologna, Modena, Parma – the Beyoncé, Rihanna, and Nicki Minaj of pasta cities.

Fun fact: this kind of dough dates back to the Middle Ages. The rich folks had chickens.

Chickens laid eggs. Boom! Egg dough was born.

Ingredients (The Real OG, for 2 people):
- 200 g "00" flour (or sifted all-purpose, if you're basic)
- 2 whole eggs (large, about 130 g total)

Step 1: Flour Fountain of Glory
Make a pile of flour on your surface and create a well like you're prepping for a chicken egg ritual. Crack both eggs into the center. Do not break the flour wall unless you want an omelet on the floor.

Step 2: Stir It Like You Mean It
Use a fork to gently beat the eggs, gradually pulling in flour from the sides. Once it stops looking like a murder scene, start kneading with your hands.

Step 3: Knead Knead Knead
Give it a solid 8–10 minutes of kneading until it becomes smooth, elastic, and slightly firm. If it's too dry, *a few drops* of water. If it's too wet, a *dusting* of flour. Don't panic. Just feel it.

Step 4: Wrap & Nap
Wrap the dough in plastic or a damp towel and let it rest for 30–60 minutes. This is sacred. Skipping the rest is like skipping foreplay. Not cool.

Step 5: Roll & Cut
Roll it out by hand or with a pasta machine to your desired thickness. Then slice into tagliatelle, fold into ravioli, or twirl into fettuccine. It's your pasta party.

Step 6: Boil Fast, Eat Slow
Cook in salty AF water. Fresh pasta cooks in minutes. Taste it early. If it melts and fights back at the same time – it's ready.

The holy trinity of pasta mother doughs

4. *GO PRO: Wanna Level Up?*
Try This Power Dough

Ingredients: Soft wheat flour (ideally "00") + a pinch of semolina flour + lots of fresh eggs

Why bother with this fickle dough? Because sometimes you want to feel like a pasta boss. This dough is richer, firmer, and golden like it spent a summer in Puglia. The added yolks bring flavor and fat, making the dough elastic and luxurious. The semolina gives it just enough backbone to stand up to any filling you throw at it, especially for tiny shapes that need to keep their cool in boiling water.

That said: she's a diva. Stiffer to knead, thirstier than your ex, and a little temperamental when it comes to resting and rolling. But once you learn how to tame her? You'll be rewarded with silky sheets and snappy folds. This is your flex pasta.

Ingredients (The Fancy Version, for 2 people):
- 200 g "00" flour (1 ⅓ cups)
- 50 g semolina flour (⅓ cup)
- 5 egg yolks (from large eggs)
- 1 whole egg (large)

Step 1: Make the volcano
Dump the "00" flour and semolina onto a clean surface (or use a big bowl if chaos isn't your thing). Mix them together, then make a well in the center.

Step 2: Add the eggs
Crack the whole egg and the yolks into the well. Use a fork to gently beat them, then slowly start pulling in flour from the sides.

Step 3: Bring it together
Once it starts to thicken, ditch the fork and go in with your hands. Knead until it forms a shaggy dough. If it feels too dry, add a few drops of water. If it's too wet, dust with more flour. You're aiming for smooth but firm.

Step 4: Knead like you mean it
Work the dough for 8-10 minutes. Yes, your arms will get tired. No, you're not allowed to quit.

Step 5: Wrap it up
Shape the dough into a ball, wrap it tightly in plastic wrap, and let it rest at room temperature for 30–60 minutes. (It needs this to chill and become rollable.)

Step 6: Use or store
After resting, your Power Dough is ready to be rolled, shaped, stuffed, and flexed on. You can also store it in the fridge for up to 24 hours, but let it come back to room temp before rolling.

The holy trinity of pasta mother doughs

A VERY BIASED GUIDE TO PASTA SHAPES BY DOUGH TYPE

A VERY BIASED GUIDE TO PASTA SHAPES BY DOUGH TYPE

Now, let's get into the formats. There are hundreds of pasta shapes. We're talking chaotic good levels of variety — every region, village, and nonna has a signature. But to make life easier, here's a totally-not-complete-but-definitely-useful list of which formats go best with which dough. Spoiler alert: it's not random. Each dough behaves differently. Some want to be rolled thin and folded like silk. Others want to be pinched, squished, or violently extruded through brass like carb Play-Doh. Let's break it down.

But First – WTF Is an Extruder?

You know those perfectly shaped penne, rigatoni, fusilli, bucatini? Yeah, you don't roll those by hand while humming opera.

They're made with an extruder: a machine that pushes stiff semolina dough through a metal die (*trafilatrice*, if you're fancy). The dies can be bronze (for rough, sauce-loving texture) or Teflon-coated (for smoother, factory-style pasta). Some are round. Some are ridged. Some are cursed. But the point is: no extruder, no penne. No bucatini. No rigatoni. Full stop.

1. Semola & Water – For Extruding, Shaping, and Sauce-Clinging Glory

Best made by hand:
- **Busiate** – long twisted spirals, usually made with a skewer and a lot of patience.
- **Cavatelli** – mini hot dog bun vibes, great with broccoli or sausage. Or both.
- **Malloreddus** – Sardinian gnocchetti with ridges for miles.
- **Orecchiette** – thumb-pressed pasta bowls. Pugliese magic.
- **Fregula** – the Italian big brother of couscous.

Best made with semolina & an extruder:
- **Bucatini** – like spaghetti, but hollow. Like your ex.
- **Fusilli** – little spirals that spin your sauce around like a pasta tornado.
- **Maccheroni** – classic short tubes, humble but dependable.
- **Penne** – slanted tubes of sauce-absorbing perfection.
- **Rigatoni** – wide, ridged tubes with "please cover me in amatriciana" energy.

Why:
Semola dough is tough, dry, and holds its shape. It's made to be extruded, pinched, dragged, or abused into form.

2. "00" Flour & Water – For Twisting, Rolling, and Zen Pasta Meditation

Best for:
- **Pici** – thick spaghetti-like ropes from Tuscany. Roll it, cut it, done.
- **Trofie** – Ligurian twists, hand-rolled and perfect for pesto.

Why:
This dough is soft and mellow. No eggs, no hard semola grip. Just water, flour, and good vibes. It's perfect for hand-shaped pasta where you want control and comfort.

3. Egg Pasta – For Folding, Filling, and Showing Off

Best for:
- **Fettuccine** – thinner ribbons for creamier sauces.
- **Lasagna sheets** – you know this one. Layer it like you layer trauma.
- **Pappardelle** – wide and dramatic, like a pasta Pavarotti.
- **Ravioli/Tortellini/Cappelletti** – filled pasta royalty. Stuff them with your dreams.
- **Tagliatelle** – classic wide ribbons, ready to drown in ragù.
- **Tagliolini/Tajarin** – ultra-thin noodles made for flexing yolk content.

Why:
Egg dough is soft, elastic, and rolls like a dream. Perfect for anything that needs to be stretched, filled, or sliced with precision.

SOME RULES OF THUMB FOR DOUGH HANDLING

Pasta may be forgiving but she still has standards. Making pasta is like dancing with the dough: you lead, it follows (until it doesn't), and the more you do it, the more your body just knows how to move. But in case your intuition hasn't kicked in yet, below are some solid starting points. Not commandments. Just humble advice from our flour-dusted kitchen to yours, designed to help you knead, slice, fold, and shape with a little more confidence.

Start by rolling your egg dough into a sheet about 1–1.5 mm thick. For tagliolini, go thinner, we're talking "can-read-through-it" thin. Dust with semola as you go, then fold the sheet like a letter. It's pasta origami, and it keeps things tidy when cutting. Use a sharp knife to slice into strips: tagliolini should be about 2–3 mm wide (delicate AF), fettuccine lands at 5 mm, tagliatelle goes bigger at 7–8 mm (Emilia-style drama), and pappardelle? As thick and wide as your soul needs.

Once cut, gently separate the strands, give them a fresh toss of semola so they don't cling to each other like needy exes, then either form little nests or lay them flat to dry. Don't skimp on the flour. Future you will be grateful.

When you're folding pockets (ravioli, tortellini, cappelletti, and so on):
For anything stuffed, your dough should be rolled very thin, again, nearing translucent. You want it strong enough to hold a filling, but light enough to melt in your mouth. Cut it into 5×5 cm squares or 6–8 cm circles depending on the shape, and add a tiny spoonful of filling. (Your enthusiasm is valid, but don't overstuff.)

Fold with love, press the edges firmly (zero air inside, please), and shape accordingly. If they burst open while boiling? That's not a pasta tragedy, that's what happens when you ignore boundaries. Respect the seal, and it will respect you back.

When you're making tubes & extruded stuff:
This is where you call in the big guns. To make true extruded pasta like rigatoni, bucatini, fusilli, and all their chunky cousins, you need an extruder. It's a machine that shoves stiff semolina dough through bronze dies like it's Play-Doh for grown-ups. Can you try to fake it by wrapping dough around a stick? Of course. Will they cook evenly or spark joy? Probably not. Some shapes simply need pressure, precision, and a lot of torque. There's a reason pasta factories sound like tiny construction zones.

Final note:
These aren't hard rules. They're strong suggestions. Think of them as your pasta training wheels. Once you've made enough mistakes (and you will), you'll get the feel for it and you can cycle through your shapes more confidently. That's when it gets fun. So break the rules when you're ready. Just don't try to make bucatini with your thumbs and a toothpick.

First things first, how to master pasta sheets:
You start with fresh egg pasta, follow the instructions on page 38.

To roll out fresh egg pasta using a pasta machine, start by dividing your dough into smaller pieces so it's easier to handle.

Flatten one piece slightly with your hands and dust it lightly with flour. Set your machine to the widest setting (usually 0 or 1) and feed the dough through once.

Fold the dough in thirds like a letter and pass it through again. Repeat this a few times to smooth it out.

Then, start narrowing the setting one step at a time, feeding the dough through each level without folding. Keep dusting with flour if it gets sticky. Stop when you reach your desired thickness: thinner for tagliolini, thicker for lasagne or stuffed pasta.

Let it rest for a couple minutes before shaping.

Step-by-step recipes

Fregula:

Toss semolina with water in a wide bowl, using your fingers to form tiny beads. Keep rolling and sprinkling until you get couscous-sized pellets. Let them dry for a bit at room temperature. Toast in the oven at 180 °C for 15 minutes (without fan), until golden and nutty – messy is normal.

Malloreddus (aka gnocchetti sardi):

Roll a small piece of semolina dough into a thin rope, about as thick as your pinky. Cut the rope into 1.5 cm (½ inch) nuggets. Roll each nugget over a ridged surface (a gnocchi board or a fork), pressing gently with your thumb. Let them curl slightly – the shape should trap sauce. No need for perfection.

*Al Dente As F*ck*

Roll your semolina dough into a rope of about 1 cm thick. Cut the rope into small sections, about the size of a coin: 1.5 cm (½ inch). Press each section flat with the tip of a butter knife or your thumb. Flip each disc inside out over your finger to form a rough-edged dome. Sauce loves the texture. Do this 200 times while rethinking your life choices.

Pici:

Grab a piece of "00" flour & water dough and roll it between your hands and the table. Stretch it out into a long, thick noodle – no knife, no machine. Aim for thicker than spaghetti, thinner than a shoelace. They need to look rustic, chunky, and 100% unapologetic.

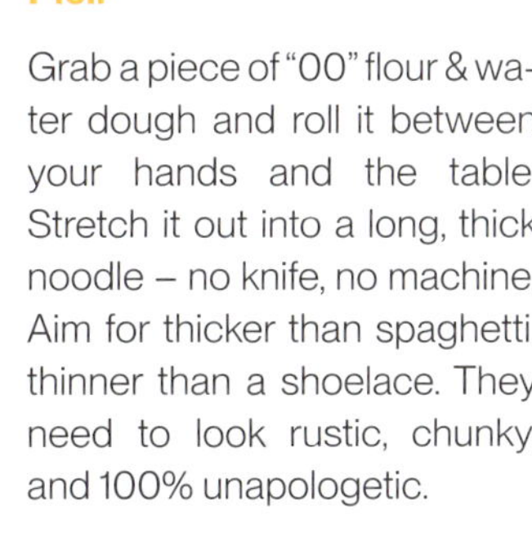

Some rules of thumb for dough handling

Take a tiny piece of "00" flour & water dough, about the size of a hazelnut. Roll it between your palm and the table to form a short, thin log. Flick or twist it lightly with your fingers or the side of your hand (the pinkie side) to create a spiral shape. Make sure it's thinner in the middle and tapered at the ends. The imperfect ones are the best.

Cappellacci:

Cut large squares of egg pasta sheet, around 6-7 cm wide, and place the filling in the center. Fold each square into a rectangle and seal the edges like a classic raviolo. Cut the edges with a fancy pasta cutter. Bring the two shorter corners (on the folded side) together and pinch them firmly. You're aiming for a crooked hat shape: big, bold, and built for ragù.

Cappelletti:

Cut your egg pasta sheet into circles using a round cutter, about 4-5 cm wide. Place a small dot of filling in the center, fold into a half-moon, and seal the edges tightly. Wrap the two tips around your finger and pinch them together to form the classic shape. They should look like little pasta hats: confident, compact, and ready for battle.

Cappelli:

Cut your pasta egg pasta sheet into large squares of around 6-7 cm, using a knife, not a cutter. Place the filling in the center, fold in half and seal the edges, keeping the top straight and flat. Bring the two bottom corners together and pinch to close, like a squared-off Cappellaccio. The final shape should scream rustic elegance – clean lines, strong energy.

Some rules of thumb for dough handling

Cut your egg pasta sheet into rectangles, about 4×7 cm. Place a small line of filling in the bottom more towards center and roll it gently like a burrito. Pinch both ends to seal, just like a wrapped candy. Optional: you can cut the wings with a fancy pasta wheel. Open the side wings for drama. They should look festive, but hold their shape like pros.

Cut your egg pasta sheet into large squares, about 6-7 cm wide. Place the filling in the center of each square. Bring all four corners up and pinch them together at the top like a gift. Seal the open sides carefully. You want plump, sealed parcels of delicious risk.

*Al Dente As F*ck*

Farfalle:

Cut your egg pasta sheet into circles using a round cutter, about 5-6 cm wide. You can also start from rectangles, but the farfalle won't look as fancy. Fold each circle gently in half, just enough to mark the center line – don't press it shut! Pinch the center of the circle between your fingers, gathering the sides into a little ruffled bowtie shape. Press firmly in the middle to seal and hold the shape. That's it, cute little farfalle, ready to party.

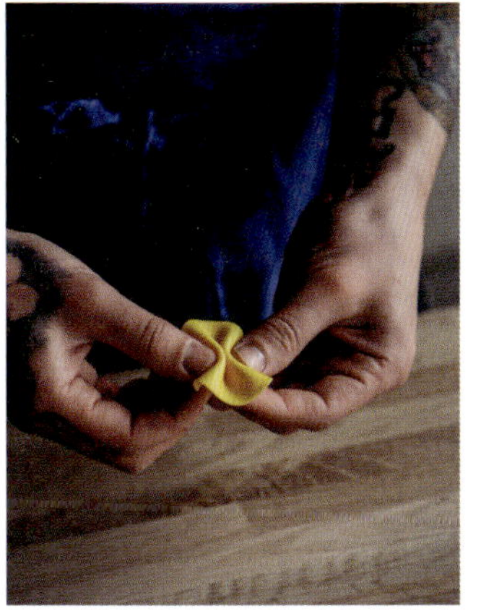

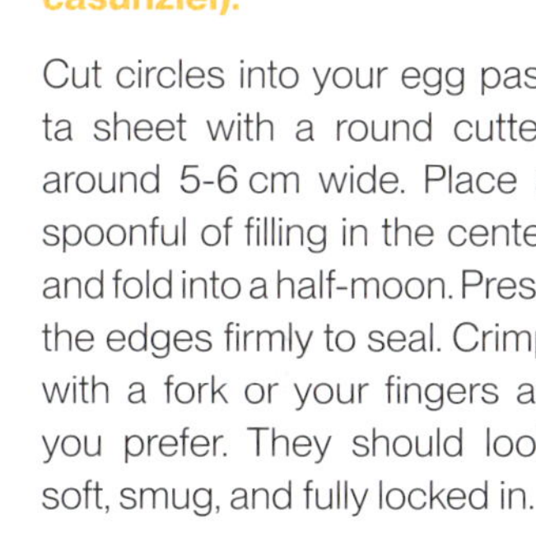

Mezzelune (aka casunziei):

Cut circles into your egg pasta sheet with a round cutter, around 5-6 cm wide. Place a spoonful of filling in the center and fold into a half-moon. Press the edges firmly to seal. Crimp with a fork or your fingers as you prefer. They should look soft, smug, and fully locked in.

Some rules of thumb for dough handling

Roll your egg dough into large, thin rectangles, about 1-2 mm thick. Trim the edges if you're in a perfectionist mood – or don't. Dust each sheet with semolina and layer between parchment paper if not using immediately. Blanch in boiling salted water for 30 seconds if baking right away. Otherwise? Layer it raw if your sauce is wet enough. Don't overthink it.

Pappardelle:

Roll your egg dough nice and thin, dust generously with sem-olina, and fold both ends multi-ple times until they meet in the middle. Cut into thick ribbons about 2 cm wide (or as *thicc* as you feel you need). Unfold each one with flair, like you're unveiling something dramatic. Toss with semola and let them shine – these aren't noodles, they're main characters.

Tagliatelle:

Roll your egg dough into a thin sheet and dust it with semolina. Fold the ends of the sheet gently, like you respect it, multiple times until they meet in the middle. Slice into ribbons about 6-8 mm wide. Unroll, toss with more semola, and fluff like you've done this a thousand times.

Tagliolini:

Roll out your egg dough super thin – think cigarette paper but edible. Dust the sheet with semolina and fold it gently like a letter. Roll both ends multiple times until they meet in the middle. Slice into fine strips, about 2-3 mm wide. Unroll the noodles, fluff with your fingers, and cook fast. They're fragile but fierce. Dress with butter, lemon, truffle, or anything bougie.

Some rules of thumb for dough handling

Roll your egg pasta into a long sheet and place small dots of filling along one half. Fold the sheet over to cover the filling, press out all the air, and seal. Cut into squares with a pasta wheel or stamp. Keep it clean and geometric. Ravioli don't need drama to be perfect.

Sorpresine:

Cut your egg pasta sheet into small squares, about 2-3 cm wide. Fold each square into a triangle, sealing only the top edges tightly. Bring the two far corners together and pinch like you're faking a tortellino. They should look fancy but hollow. Fast to cook, fun to eat, pure *delulu*.

Tortellini:

Cut your egg pasta sheet into squares of about 3-4 cm wide. Place a tiny dot of filling in the center, fold into a triangle, and seal the edges well. Wrap the triangle around your fingertip and pinch the two tips together. If it looks like a little bellybutton, you nailed it.

Tortellacci:

Cut large circles of your egg pasta sheet, using a round cutter about 6-7 cm wide. Add a generous spoonful of filling, fold into a half-moon, and seal the edge tightly. Fold the curved edge slightly inward, then bring the two corners toward you. Pinch them together like a smile – it should look like the gym bro of a tortellino.

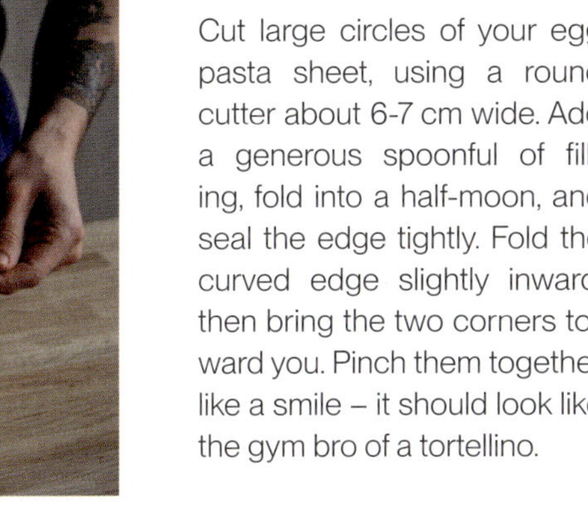

Some rules of thumb for dough handling

HOW TO NOT
RUIN EVERYTHING
YOU JUST MADE

HOW TO NOT RUIN EVERYTHING YOU JUST MADE

This is your pasta advice column. Here, we take your tales of soggy woe and turn them into teaching moments. Or: better luck next time. Pasta has a cruel sense of humor, punishing tiny mistakes with disproportionate disaster. Overcook it by a minute, and it's mush. Drain it too soon, and the sauce won't stick to it. Heat matters, timing matters, salt matters. Hours of effort can vanish faster than a chunk of parmesan in a hungry crowd. We're here to help.

First, What Not to Do – or: Common Beginner Fails

1. **"I didn't rest the dough, it seemed fine."**
   Yeah, and your ex seemed nice too. Resting the dough = gluten relaxing = dough that rolls out like butter. No rest? It'll snap back like a rubber band and your shapes will look like abstract art.

2. **"I added too much flour while kneading."**
   Congrats, you made shortbread. Your dough should feel firm but elastic, not like sidewalk chalk. It's okay if it's a *bit* sticky at first. Better sticky than dusty.

3. **"I eyeballed the water/egg ratio."**
   Why. Would. You. Do. That. Use a scale. Pasta dough isn't the place to "vibe it out". Unless you want to vibe your way into a gluey disaster.

4. **"I rolled it thick because I like it rustic."**
   No. Rustic ≠ raw. If you can patch drywall with your pasta, it's too thick. Aim for transparency. If you can read cuss words through it, it's perfect.

5. **"I skipped sealing my ravioli properly."**
   And now your filling is floating in the pot like a lost soul in purgatory. Press out all the air, seal the edges *tight*, and use a little water if needed. If it bursts in the water, that's a ravioli homicide and it's on you.

6. **"I made a giant batch without testing first."**
   Slow down, chef. Make a small batch, cook one or two, taste, adjust. Better to fail on four tagliatelle than forty.

7. **"I left the pasta out while I made the sauce."**
   Guess what? It dried into a sculpture. Fresh pasta dries FAST. If you're not cooking it right away, cover it with a damp cloth or wrap it. Or just toss it and start over. (Sorry.)

8. **"I didn't flour the ribbons enough."**
   Now you've got one big sticky lasagna monster. Dust your pasta with semola after cutting. Gently separate the strands like you're diffusing a bomb.

9. **"I overcooked it just to be safe."**
   You boiled it to death. It's gone. Fresh pasta cooks fast. No excuses. Taste it early.

10. **"I followed a TikTok video instead of a proper recipe."**
    If your dough had avocado in it, or food coloring, or used a hair straightener, we can't help you. Nobody can help you. Try therapy.

Second, the Ten Pasta Rules to Live By

1. **Flour It. Wrap It. Don't Screw It Up.**
    Dust your pasta with semola grossa, not regular flour. It won't gum up and keeps everything light and sexy. Don't go full Sahara: just enough to stop it sticking, don't start exfoliating. If you're not using it right away, wrap it tight in plastic or cover with a damp towel so it doesn't dry out. Humidity = elasticity. Crusty dough is dead dough. Treat it like a superstar: powder it, wrap it up in a nice jacket, and treat it as high maintenance.

2. **Salt Your Water Like You're Poseidon.**
    If your pasta water tastes like tears of the Adriatic? Perfect. If it tastes like a British summer? Start over. Ratio: 10 g of salt per liter of water. Yes, really. Pasta without salt is sadness incarnate.

3. **Big Pot. Rolling Boil. No Weak Bubbles.**
    Pasta needs space. Boil it in a pot big enough to bathe a small dog. If your water slows down to a sad simmer when you drop the pasta in, it's too cold. Wait for the angry boil before you start.

4. **Don't Dump It and Walk Away**
    Fresh pasta cooks FAST. Like, 60–120 seconds. You don't have time to text your ex or open Instagram. Stay. Taste. Watch. Overcooked pasta = a culinary capital crime.

5. **Stir It. Right Away. Always.**
    Especially If you've got ribbons or filled pasta. Pasta wants to stick together like toxic friendships. Break it up early with a gentle stir.

6. **Save Your Pasta Water Like It's Liquid Gold.**
    Scoop out a cup before you drain. It's starchy, salty magic and makes your sauce *actually cling* instead of slide off like a toddler's attention span. Use it to emulsify, thin out, or save a sauce gone too thick.

7. **Don't Rinse It. Don't You Dare.**
    Rinsing pasta = rinsing off flavor and starch. The only time this is allowed is if you're making pasta for a cold salad – and even then, we're still judging you a little.

8. **Don't Let It Sit Around Naked.**
    Pasta waiting alone in a bowl = tragedy. Toss it with sauce immediately or at least oil it up to prevent sticking. Pasta dries out and clumps faster than a group chat after midnight.

9. **Don't Drown It in Sauce.**
    Pasta is the main character, not a spoon rest for sauce. Balance. Emulsion. A little sauce clinging to every bite, not a swimming pool of sludge. *We're not making soup.*

10. **Eat It Now. Not Later. NOW.**
    Fresh pasta waits for no one. Not your friends, not your date, not your ego. It's at its best minutes after cooking. So plate it, serve it, and watch the room go quiet. That's your moment.

TRADITIONAL
RECIPES — JUST
NOT LIKE YOUR
NONNA MADE THEM

MALLOREDDUS WITH GREEN ASPARAGUS & ANCHOVY GLOW-UP

A Sardinian classic gets a spring makeover. Creamy asparagus, crispy tips, and anchovies dropped in like salty plot twists. Totally addictive.

Ingredients

300 g malloreddus (~2 cups/10.6 oz dry) (see page 48)
400 g green asparagus, ends trimmed (~2 cups cut/10.6 oz)
olive oil, liberal drizzle (~3 tbsp/1.5 oz)
60 ml heavy cream (~4 tbsp/2 oz)
60–90 ml pasta cooking water (4–6 tbsp/2–3 oz), reserved
6–9 high-quality anchovy fillets in oil (~30 g/~1 oz total)
salt & black pepper to taste
optional: lemon zest or chili flakes

How to Make It

Prep the asparagus like you mean it. Snap off woody ends, separate tips from stems. Slice stems thinly.

Cook stems until they give up. Heat olive oil, toss stems with a pinch of salt. Add 4–6 tbsp water and cook low for 5–10 minutes until falling apart. Add small splashes of water if needed.

Make it creamy. Blend stems with heavy cream. You want smooth, velvety sauce. Season to taste.

Pan-roast the asparagus tips. In a separate pan, heat 1 tbsp (0.5 oz) olive oil. Sear tips until golden. Lightly salt.

Boil the malloreddus. In a large pot of heavily salted water (~10 g/0.3 oz salt per liter), cook the malloreddus for 8–10 minutes until al dente. Reserve some pasta water before draining.

Toss it all together. Warm the asparagus cream sauce in a pan, add drained pasta, toss. Add reserved pasta water to help emulsify.

Plate it like you care. Serve with seared asparagus tips, and top with anchovy fillets. Optional sass: finish with lemon zest or chili flakes if you're feeling fancy.

ORECCHIETTE WITH SAUSAGE & RAPINI

Straight outta Puglia, this combo is pure comfort. Bitter greens, juicy sausage, and chewy orecchiette that catch all the goodness. It's the kind of dish that doesn't ask, it tells you to sit down and eat.

Ingredients

420 g cime di rapa/rapini, cleaned and trimmed
    (~5 cups chopped/14.8 oz)
300 g fresh orecchiette (~2 cups/10.6 oz) (see page 49)
120 ml pasta cooking water (1/2 cup/4 oz), reserved
2 tbsp olive oil (~45 ml/1.5 oz)
2 garlic cloves, smashed
1 small chili pepper, or a pinch of flakes
250 g Italian sausage, skinned (~1 2/3 cup crumbled/8.8 oz)
salt to taste
optional: Pecorino to finish, if you're feeling frisky

How to Make It

Prep the greens. Clean the rapini: remove tough stalks, keep the tender leaves and florets. Chop roughly. Don't overthink it.

Blanch the greens like a boss. Boil in salted water for 3–5 minutes until tender but still green. Drain and *squeeze out excess water*. You don't want swamp vibes in your sauce.

Boil your pasta. In a large pot of heavily salted water, cook the orecchiette until al dente. Save some pasta water before draining. Always.

Sauté the sausage. In a big-ass pan, heat 2 tbsp olive oil, add garlic and chili, then the sausage. Break the sausage up with a wooden spoon. Cook until golden and crisp in spots. *This is not steamed sausage hour.*

Add the greens. Toss in the blanched rapini and stir. Let it all vibe together for a couple minutes. If it looks dry? Splash in a bit of that reserved pasta water.

Unite the carb kingdom. Drain the pasta and toss it straight into the pan. Add a bit more pasta water and stir until everything's glossy and gorgeous. NO cream, NO butter. Just emulsify with some elbow grease.

Plate it. Eat it. Serve immediately and ignore anyone who says "This would be nice with cream." Top with grated pecorino if you want extra attitude.

TROFIE AL PESTO WITH POTATOES & GREEN BEANS

Ligurian core. Soft potatoes, crunchy beans, twisty pasta – tied together by that pesto. It's green, it's bouncy, it's basically edible sunshine.

Ingredients

160 g potatoes, peeled and diced small (~ 1 cup/5.8 oz)
100 g green beans, trimmed and cut into 3–4 cm pieces
      (~1 cup/3.5 oz)
300 g fresh trofie (~2 cups/10.6 oz) (see page 50)
130 g pesto Genovese (~1/2 cup/4.5 oz) (see page 149)
salt, for the water
120 ml pasta cooking water (1/2 cup/4 oz), as needed
optional: fresh basil leaves, Parmigiano Reggiano or
      Pecorino, grated

How to Make It

Boil the potatoes and beans. In a big pot of salty water, add the diced potatoes. After 2–3 minutes, add the green beans. After 5 more minutes, they should be just tender. Don't overcook them into mushy sadness.

Add the pasta straight into the same pot. Toss the trofie into the water with the veg. Cook everything together until the pasta is al dente. Pro move: scoop out some of that starchy liquid gold before draining.

Drain fast, toss faster. As soon as the pasta is cooked, drain everything (gently), and toss immediately with your pesto Genovese in a big bowl. Add a spoonful or two of pasta water to help loosen and gloss it up – no heat! Never cook pesto. It's a sauce, not a stew.

Stir like you mean it. Stir until everything's coated and creamy – but not soupy. You want it to hug, not drown.

Plate with optional drama. Add a tear of extra basil on top if you're theatrical. A spoonful of grated Parm or Pecorino? Sure. Purists may scream, but your mouth won't.

*Al Dente As F*ck*

PICI ALLE BRICIOLE

Tuscany's peasant masterpiece. Thick hand-rolled noodles tossed in garlicky breadcrumbs like they own the place. Proof that "poor" food can still taste rich.

Ingredients

300 g fresh pici (~2 cups/10.6 oz) (see page 49)
100 g stale bread, grated or blitzed into crumbs (~1 2/3 cup/3.5 oz)
3-4 garlic cloves, thinly sliced
60 ml olive oil (~4 tbsp/2 oz)
optional: 1 small chili (or a pinch of flakes); fresh parsley, chopped
    (~1 ½ tbsp/5 g/0.2 oz)
salt, to taste
120 ml pasta cooking water (1/2 cup/4 oz), as needed

How to Make It

Boil the pasta. Drop the pici into a big pot of salty, angry, boiling water. Cook until al dente. Save some pasta water before draining.

Toast the breadcrumbs like they owe you money. In a dry pan, toast the crumbs over medium heat until golden and crunchy – about 5 minutes. Stir often so they don't burn. Remove and set aside like they're VIPs.

Sizzle the garlic. In the same pan, add olive oil, then the garlic slices (and chili if using). Fry gently until golden and fragrant, not burnt. If they go brown, *start over*. Garlic drama is never worth it.

Bring the party together. Add the cooked pici directly into the garlic oil. Toss with a splash of pasta water to coat everything. Add half the toasted crumbs and stir. You want clingy, crispy, shiny glory.

Plate & crown with crumbs. Divide into bowls and top with the remaining breadcrumbs for texture. Add chopped parsley if you're feeling green. No cheese. Don't even ask. This is *breadcrumb supremacy*.

*Al Dente As F*ck*

FREGULA WITH CLAMS, 'NDUJA & LEMON ZEST

One forkful of this zingy, spicy seaside in a bowl, and you'll be hooked like a Sardinian fish. Line and sinker.

Ingredients

1 kg fresh clams, purged (~2 lb/8 cups in-shell)
2 tbsp olive oil (~30 ml/1 oz)
1 garlic clove, smashed
300 g fregula sarda (~1 ¾ cup/10.6 oz) (see page 48)
hot water or light fish stock, to cook the fregula
     (~1 liter/4 cups/34 oz)
45 g 'nduja (~2 heaping tbsp/~1.7 oz)
zest of 1 lemon
optional: white wine, a splash (~30 ml/1 oz); fresh parsley,
     chopped (~1 tbsp/3 g/0.1 oz)
salt & black pepper, to taste

How to Make It

Clean the clams, no excuses. Rinse well, purge in salted water at least 30 minutes. Toss any open or broken ones. We love seafood, not salmonella.

Start with flavor. In a wide pan, heat olive oil and smash in that garlic clove. Add a splash of white wine (if using) and the clams. Cover and cook for 2–3 minutes until they pop open. Remove clams and strain the liquid – save it. It's liquid gold.

Cook the fregula like risotto. In the same pan, toast the fregula for 1–2 minutes. Add the clam juice and hot water or fish stock one ladle at a time, stirring often. Cook gently for 8–10 minutes, until al dente and brothy-creamy. If it's drying out, add more liquid. We want cozy, not crunchy.

Drop the 'nduja in. When the fregula is nearly ready, melt in the 'nduja and stir. Let it perfume the whole thing – not dominate, just seduce.

Clams go back in. Add the cooked clams (in or out of shell; your aesthetic choice) and toss everything together. Taste for salt – between clams and 'nduja, you may need zero.

Zest and bless. Finish with fresh lemon zest, a grind of black pepper, and chopped parsley if you're that kind of person. Serve immediately. Spoon it. Slurp it. Fall in love.

*Al Dente As F*ck*

TAGLIOLINI BURRO E LIEVITO

Call it vegan adjacent, call it buttered noodles with flair — either way, this hits hard. Umami-packed, cheesy and rich without trying too hard.

Ingredients

300 g fresh tagliolini (~2 ⅓ cups/10.6 oz) (see page 55)
65 g unsalted butter (~3 tbsp/1.4 oz)
60 g nutritional yeast flakes (~3 tbsp/1.2 oz)*
salt & black pepper, to taste
180 ml pasta cooking water (3/4 cup/6 oz), as needed

How to Make It

Cook the tagliolini in salty water. Not "a pinch" salty. Sea-level salty. Fresh tagliolini cook in minutes, so don't you dare walk away. Scoop out some pasta water before draining.

Melt the butter like a love letter. In a large pan, melt butter over low heat until it foams gently. No browning. Just melted and silky.

Add pasta + yeast + water = sauce magic. Toss in the drained tagliolini, add nutritional yeast and pasta water, one spoonful at a time. Stir like you're building an emulsion (because you are). The sauce should coat every strand: shiny, velvety, a little cheeky.

Season and plate. Add salt if needed (the yeast is savory, so taste first), crack on some black pepper. Plate like it's more than buttered noodles. Because it is. Optional flex: another micro-sprinkle of yeast on top for full umami chaos.

***What the Hell Is Nutritional Yeast
(aka "lievito in fiocchi")?**
No, it's not the stuff you use to make pizza rise, and no, it's not going to explode in your stomach. Nutritional yeast is an inactive yeast, meaning it's dead, chill, and just here to party with your taste buds. It comes in golden-yellow flakes, looks kinda like fish food, and tastes like a love child between Parmesan and toasted nuts with a secret umami agenda. It's vegan, high in B-vitamins, and weirdly addictive. You'll find it in health food stores, online, or anywhere that sells overpriced almonds. Here, we're not using it for health — we're using it for FLAVOR. It melts into butter and turns your pasta into *low-effort, high-impact* umami gold.

*Al Dente As F*ck*

TAGLIATELLE WITH CLASSIC RAGÙ ALLA BOLOGNESE

Serves 2 people with good taste and zero patience for fake bolognese.

Straight out of Bologna, no shortcuts allowed. Slow-cooked meat sauce, fresh egg pasta – this is Italy's version of "don't mess with perfection."

Ingredients

3 tbsp olive oil or butter (~45 ml/1.5 oz)
85 g pancetta, finely chopped (~1/2 cup/3 oz)
50 g onion, finely diced (~⅓ cup/1.8 oz)
50 g carrot, finely diced (~⅓ cup/1.8 oz)
50 g celery, finely diced (~⅓ cup/1.8 oz)
250 g ground beef (preferably chuck) (~1 2/3 cup/8.8 oz)
100 ml red wine (~ ⅓ cup/3.4 oz)
1 tbsp tomato paste (~20 g/0.7 oz)
100 ml passata di pomodoro (~ ⅓ cup/3.4 oz)
optional: a tiny splash of broth or warm water if it dries out
100 ml whole milk (~⅓ cup/3.4 oz)
300 g fresh tagliatelle (~2 ¼ cups/10.6 oz) (see page 55)
Parmigiano Reggiano, grated, to finish

How to Make It (Respectfully)

Start with the pancetta. In a saucepan, heat olive oil or butter, then toss in the chopped pancetta and let it render gently for 2-3 minutes. If it smells like Sunday, you're doing it right.

Add the veg. Add the onion, carrot, and celery to the pancetta and sauté over medium-low heat until soft but not browned (about 8-10 minutes).

Time for the beef. Add the ground chuck and break it up with a wooden spoon. Cook slowly until well browned – no gray meat allowed. This step takes time. Respect it.

Deglaze. Pour in the red wine, let it bubble and reduce until the alcohol is gone and the pan smells divine.

Tomato it up. Stir in the tomato paste and passata. Don't drown the meat. This is ragù, not red sauce cosplay.

Simmer like you love it. Add a splash of warm water or light broth to loosen it up if needed. Let it simmer uncovered, super low heat, for at least one hour (ideally longer). Stir occasionally, talk to it nicely.

Add the milk near the end. Pour in milk during the last 15–20 minutes of cooking. It balances acidity, makes everything velvety, and yes, it's essential.

Cook the pasta, marry the two. Boil tagliatelle in salty water until al dente. Toss straight into the ragù. Stir gently until each ribbon is coated like it got dressed for a gala.

Serve hot, top with Parmigiano, and shut up. That's it. No basil. No garlic. Just pure, quiet joy.

Emanuele's Note

Okay okay – we gave you the official Bolognese. But if you're cooking in our kitchen? Here's what we do: we like to add a bit of sausage with fennel seed (just a small amount, like 50–70g/2–2.5 oz) along with the ground beef. It adds extra depth and a whisper of wildness. Just enough to make your palate go "Wait, what was that?" The structure stays classic. The flavor becomes ours. Try it once. You'll never go back.

*Al Dente As F*ck*

PAPPARDELLE WITH WILD BOAR RAGÙ

Hunting season in a bowl. Big, bold ribbons meet slow-braised wild boar in a sauce that tastes like Tuscany in November. It's primal. It's poetic. It's perfect.

Ingredients

300 g wild boar meat, diced small (~2 cups/10.6 oz)
150 ml dry red wine (~⅔ cup/5 oz)
2 garlic cloves, smashed
1 sprig rosemary
1 bay leaf
3 tbsp olive oil (~45 ml/1.5 oz)
½ carrot, finely chopped (~30 g/¼ cup/1.1 oz)
½ celery stalk, finely chopped (~30 g/¼ cup/1.1 oz)
½ onion, finely chopped (~50 g/⅓ cup/1.8 oz)
salt & pepper to taste
1 tbsp tomato paste (~20 g/0.7 oz)
200 ml water or game stock (~¾ cup + 1 tbsp/6.8 oz)
2–3 juniper berries, lightly crushed
optional: 1 tsp grated dark chocolate (yes, seriously)
300 g fresh pappardelle (~2 ¼ cups/10.6 oz) (see page 54)

How to Make It

Marinate the boar (optional but iconic). If you have time, marinate the diced wild boar in red wine with a clove of garlic, rosemary, and bay leaf for a few hours or overnight. Drain before cooking and pat dry. This step turns "good" into *epic*.

Make the soffritto. In a deep pan, heat the olive oil. Add carrot, celery, onion, garlic, and rosemary. Sauté on low heat until soft and golden – no rushing.

Brown the meat like a legend. Add the boar meat, season with salt and pepper, and brown it thoroughly on all sides. This is where the flavor builds. Make it count.

Deglaze with red wine. Add wine, scrape the bottom, and let it reduce by half. The pan should smell like *hunt and poetry*.

Tomato time. Stir in the tomato paste. Add water or stock to cover about ¾ of the meat. Add bay leaf and juniper. Simmer low, half-covered, for up to two hours. Add splashes of water as needed.

Secret move. Optional but game-changing: stir in a teaspoon of grated dark chocolate at the very end. It doesn't make it taste like dessert – it just deepens the whole thing like a Tuscan forest after the rain.

Boil the pappardelle. Big pot, salty water, 3–4 minutes if fresh. Drain and toss with the ragù, no holding back. If it needs help binding: pasta water magic.

Plate it like you live in a stone house on a hill. A big bowl. A fork. A glass of red wine. Don't even *think* about cheese.

SORPRESINE WITH SWEET PEA CREAM, GOAT CHEESE & CAPER FLOWERS

A soft, herby mix wrapped in tiny pasta hugs, topped with a pea cream and briny caper flowers. Fresh, light, and just a little bit flirty. Looks simple but tastes like green luxury.

Ingredients

300 g sorpresine (~2 ¼ cups/10.6 oz) (see page 56)
For the pea cream:
200 g peas, boiled (~1 ⅓ cup/7 oz)
100 g soft goat cheese (~1/2 cup/3.5 oz)
2 tbsp olive oil (~30 ml/1 oz)
salt & pepper, to taste
optional: lemon zest for brightness
To finish:
1 tbsp butter (~15 g/0.5 oz)
130 g peas, blanched (~1 cup/4.6 oz)
extra pasta water, as needed
12–16 caper flowers, rinsed
optional: lemon zest or fresh herbs

How to Make It

Make the pea cream. Blend the boiled peas with goat cheese and olive oil until smooth and silky. Season with salt, pepper, and lemon zest if you're feeling fancy.

Boil the pasta in salty water until al dente. Fresh pasta = 3–4 minutes, you know the drill by now. Save some of that pasta water. Always.

Melt the butter in a pan. Toss in the cooked sorpresine with the whole peas and a bit of pasta water. Take off the heat, stir in the pea cream until everything is glossy and green.

Plate it. Lay down that creamy, bright sauce. Add the sorpresine, scatter whole peas, and crown with caper flowers like you're plating spring itself.

Traditional recipes – just not like your nonna made them

FARFALLE WITH SAFFRON & BONE MARROW

Risotto alla milanese, but make it pasta. Golden saffron cream, roasted bone marrow, and bows fancy enough for aperitivo at La Scala. Milan said "butter". We said "make it fashion".

Ingredients

1 small pinch of saffron threads (~0.1 g/just over 1/16 tsp)
2 tbsp hot water (~30 ml/1 oz)
2 marrow bones or about 130 g marrow removed (~1/2 cup/2.5 oz)
1 shallot, finely chopped (~50 g/⅓ cup/1.7 oz)
20 g butter (~1 ½ tbsp/0.7 oz)
100 ml heavy cream (~⅓ cup + 1 tbsp/3.4 oz)
300 g fresh farfalle all'uovo (~2 ¼ cups/10.6 oz) (see page 53)
salt & white pepper, to taste
optional: Parmigiano Reggiano, very finely grated; extra salt flakes
and a blowtorch, for maximum Milanese drama

How to Make It

Prep the saffron. Steep the threads in hot water for at least 15 minutes. Gold takes time.

Roast the bone marrow. If using bones: roast them upright in a hot oven (200°C/400°F) for 15 minutes. Scoop out the marrow. If already extracted: roast it in a small dish, then hit it with a blowtorch at the end for color and chef's swagger. Blowtorch optional. Attitude mandatory.

Make the sauce. Sauté the shallot in butter until soft and translucent. Add the saffron infusion and let it reduce slightly. Stir in the cream, let it thicken gently. Salt and pepper to taste.

Cook the farfalle in salty water until al dente. Drain and toss in the saffron cream. Add a spoonful of pasta water if it needs loosening up.

Spoon the golden farfalle onto warm plates. Top each portion with blobs of roasted marrow. If you're feeling reckless: a little Parmigiano and a sprinkle of sea salt flakes.

Al Dente As F*ck

SPINACH & RICOTTA RAVIOLI WITH LEMON BUTTER

The poster child of stuffed pasta. Delicate green filling, melty lemon butter, and just enough nutmeg to make it smell like Sunday at nonna's. This one's a hug. A citrusy, buttery, herby hug.

Ingredients

150 g cooked spinach, well drained and chopped (~1 cup/5.3 oz)
150 g ricotta (~⅔ cup/5.3 oz)
30 g Parmigiano Reggiano, grated (~¼ cup/1 oz)
1 small egg yolk
salt, black pepper, and nutmeg, to taste
200 g fresh pasta sheets (~1 ½ cups/7 oz) (see page 56)
100 g butter (~7.5 tbsp/3.5 oz)
zest of 1 small lemon
baby spinach leaves, to finish
optional: squeeze of lemon juice or Parmigiano, to finish

How to Make It

Make the filling. Mix spinach (well squeezed), ricotta, Parmigiano, egg yolk, salt, pepper, and a grating of nutmeg. It should be creamy but firm enough to hold its shape.

Roll out the pasta sheets. As per the instructions on page 56. Cut into squares, pipe or spoon filling in the center, close with another square, press edges well. No air bubbles or leaky ravioli, please. We're classy today.

Boil in salty water. For 5 minutes or until just al dente. Don't overcook them. They're softies.

Make the sauce. While they boil, melt butter in a pan until foamy and just starting to brown. Add lemon zest right at the end so it stays fragrant, not bitter.

Toss & plate. Gently coat the ravioli in the lemon butter. Finish with a little extra zest, Parm if you're feeling it, and baby leaves on top for the drama.

Traditional recipes – just not like your nonna made them

*Al Dente As F*ck*

TORTELLINI IN CAPON BROTH

Tiny meat-filled halos swimming in golden capon broth. It's not just a dish — it's a religion. Best served hot, loud, and surrounded by family yelling across the table. This is a rite of passage.

Ingredients

1 medium capon (~2.5–3 kg/5.5–6.5 lb), jointed
substitute with chicken, if you're a law-abiding citizen
2 carrots
2 celery stalks
1 onion, halved (*optional:* lightly charred for depth)
1 bay leaf
3–5 whole black peppercorns
2–3 whole cloves
50 g pork loin, cooked in butter and cooled (~⅓ cup/1.8 oz)
50 g prosciutto crudo, finely chopped (~⅓ cup/1.8 oz)
50 g mortadella di Bologna, finely chopped (~⅓ cup/1.8 oz)
75 g Parmigiano Reggiano, finely grated (~½ cup/2.6 oz)
1 small egg
nutmeg, freshly grated, to taste
200 g fresh egg pasta, shaped into tortellini (~1 ½ cups/7 oz)
(see page 57)
cold water, enough to cover (about 3–3.5 liter/12–14 cups)
salt, to taste

How to Make It

Start the broth, liquid gold, soul fuel. Worth every hour. In a large pot, combine the capon, vegetables, spices, and cold water. Bring it slowly to a simmer – no boiling. Skim off any foam or impurities that rise to the top. Let it bubble away for 3–4 hours, uncovered, on low heat. Patience is nonna's secret weapon. Once done, strain the broth and chill it if making ahead. Skim off the fat layer before reheating.

Make the filling. No tweaks, no shortcuts. Sauté the pork loin in a bit of butter, cool it down. Once cold, mix it thoroughly with the prosciutto, mortadella, Parmigiano, egg, nutmeg, and salt. You want a savory, cohesive filling that holds its shape. Chill it before using. Everything should be chopped *super fine* – either by knife like a true artisan or carefully blitzed in a food processor (don't overdo it). The texture should be dense and compact, not mousse-like.

Shape the tortellini. As per the instructions on page 57. Roll your pasta dough as thin as humanly possible. Cut into squares of 3x3 cm/1.2x1.2 in. Add a tiny dab of filling. Fold into triangles, then wrap around your finger to seal that classic bellybutton shape.

Cook in broth. Heat the capon broth until gently boiling. Drop in the tortellini. Cook for 4–5 minutes, until they float. They should be tender but hold their shape, no disintegrating soldiers allowed.

Ladle into wide bowls. Serve hot. No black pepper, no fancy oil, no "creative twists." Just tortellini and broth. Optional rebel move: a sprinkle of Parmigiano. But don't tell the purists.

Bruna's Note

Here's a fun fact: Italians are obsessed with capon broth. Regular chicken broth is for Tuesdays. Capon broth is what you bring out when the Pope's coming over or it's Christmas Eve and your nonna is judging your life choices. Capon (a castrated rooster – illegal to rear in some countries) is fattier and richer than your regular chicken, and it builds the kind of broth that coats your mouth, heals your trauma, and probably lowers your taxes. It's the secret weapon of every serious holiday table from Emilia to Campania.

Traditional recipes – just not like your nonna made them

*Al Dente As F*ck*

CAPPELLETTI WITH WHITE ASPARAGUS CREAM & CRISPY PANCETTA

Spring luxury in pasta form. Stuffed with white asparagus and ricotta, finished with cream and crispy pancetta. Elegant but still ready to party. Delicate but no wallflower.

Ingredients

For the filling:

120 g white asparagus, peeled (~3/4 cups/4.2 oz)
100 g ricotta (~½ cup/3.5 oz)
1 tbsp breadcrumbs (~8 g/0.3 oz)
salt & black pepper, to taste

For the sauce:

200 g white asparagus, peeled (~1 ½ cups/7 oz)
1 tbsp olive oil (~15 ml/0.5 oz)
2–3 tbsp pasta water or vegetable broth, to blend
salt & white pepper, to taste
60 g pancetta, cubed or sliced (~½ cup/2.1 oz)
1 tbsp butter (~15 g/0.5 oz)
200 g fresh egg pasta, shaped into cappelletti (~1 ½ cups/7 oz)
   (see page 51)
optional: lemon zest or Parmigiano, for that extra *glow up*

How to Make It

Make the asparagus filling. Separate stems from tips. Chop the stems, save the tips. Boil the chopped asparagus stems until soft. Blend to a smooth purée, mix with ricotta, breadcrumbs, salt and pepper. Add Parmigiano and lemon zest if using. Chill the filling so it firms up.

Shape the cappelletti. As per the instructions on page 51. Classic fold: square to triangle, pinch the corners together. Make them small, neat, and smug.

Make the sauce. Boil or sauté the asparagus stalks in olive oil until soft, then blend with pasta water or broth until creamy and smooth. Season well – white asparagus is subtle, it needs a push.

Crisp the pancetta in a hot pan until golden. Add the asparagus tips for the last minute to lightly sauté in the fat. Remove from heat, swirl in the butter for that glossy finish.

Cook the cappelletti in salty water. For 2–3 minutes until they float. Toss gently with the asparagus cream to coat.

Plate like a pro. Spoon the creamy sauce into warm plates, arrange the cappelletti, and scatter over pancetta and asparagus tips. Extra lemon zest and Parm, if you want it.

Emanuele's Note

You can bump up the cheese if you're feeling bold – even add a spoonful of Pecorino for extra sass. Just don't drown the asparagus. It's asparagus with cheese, not cheese with a hazy memory of asparagus.

CAPPELLACCI DI MORTADELLA WITH CREAM SAUCE

Bologna in silk pajamas. Delicate pasta hugs mortadella, all dressed up in a silky cream sauce that feels like a warm hug… from a butcher. Pure mortadella glory.

Ingredients

120 g mortadella di Bologna, finely chopped (~¾ cup/4.2 oz)
100 g ricotta (~½ cup/3.5 oz)
30 g Parmigiano Reggiano, grated (~¼ cup/1 oz)
1 tbsp breadcrumbs (~8 g/0.3 oz)
Grating of nutmeg, to taste
salt & pepper, optional (taste your mortadella – it's already
    seasoned)
200 g fresh egg pasta, shaped into cappellacci (~1 ½ cups/7 oz)
    (see page 50)
450 ml heavy cream (~2 cups/15 oz)
45 g butter (~3 tbsp/1.5 oz)
optional: a crack of white pepper, tiny zest of lemon, or Parmigiano,
    finely grated

How to Make It

Make the filling. Finely chop the mortadella (by hand or pulse in a mixer – but don't turn it into mush). Mix with ricotta, Parmigiano, breadcrumbs, nutmeg. Chill. It should taste like you want to eat it straight from the bowl with a spoon. Because you will.

Roll out the pasta & shape the cappellacci. As per the instructions on page 50. Cappellacci = *big boi* tortelloni folded with flair. Think "pasta origami but sexy".

Cook the cappellacci al dente. In salted water for 4–5 minutes, or until done.

Reduce the cream sauce gently while the pasta cooks. Heat gently until just thickened and warm. No boiling, no separating, no drama. The sauce should coat the pasta, not drown it. Add a knob of butter, stir slowly.

Toss and serve. Drain cappellacci, toss in the cream sauce, plate with finesse. Optional finishing touch: a zest of lemon, some cracked white pepper or Parm dust. But honestly? They're already perfect, just the way they are.

TORTELLACCI WITH RICOTTA, PEARS, WALNUTS & GORGONZOLA SAUCE

Sweet meets salty in this northern icon. Buttery pears, crunchy walnuts, creamy cheese — wrapped in pasta and drowned in melted blue chaos. A soft, sweet, salty, chaotic love story.

Ingredients

100 g ricotta (~½ cup/3.5 oz)
1 ripe pear, peeled and finely diced (~100 g/¾ cup/3.5 oz)
30 g walnuts, toasted and chopped (~¼ cup/1 oz)
20 g Parmigiano Reggiano, grated (~2 tbsp/0.7 oz)
1 tbsp breadcrumbs (~8 g/0.3 oz)
salt & white pepper, to taste
200 g fresh egg pasta, shaped into tortellacci (~1 ½ cups/7 oz)
     (see page 57)
180 g Gorgonzola Dolce (~3/4 cup/5 oz)
200 ml heavy cream (~3/4 cup/4 oz)
20 g butter (~1 ½ tbsp/0.7 oz)
optional: chopped walnuts, extra slivers of pear, Parmigiano flakes

How to Make It

Make the filling. Combine ricotta, diced pear, chopped walnuts, Parmigiano, breadcrumbs, and seasoning. Taste it. Sigh a little. Chill it. The filling should be creamy but not wet. We're not making smoothies here. For extra magic, sauté the diced pear in a little butter until just lightly caramelized: golden edges, soft center, still holding shape. It brings out the sweetness and stops your filling from turning into sad pear soup. You want the pear to keep its shape as little juicy bits, not turn to mush.

Roll out the pasta and shape the tortellacci. As per the instructions on page 57. Tortellacci = like tortelloni but bigger and with more attitude. You're going for statement pasta energy.

Make the sauce. Melt Gorgonzola, cream, and butter together. Very low heat, because Gorgonzola has a fragile ego. Stir until smooth and pourable. The sauce should hug, not drown.

Cook the tortellacci in salty water. 4–5 minutes should do it.

Plate & flex. Spoon the gorgonzola sauce onto plates and gently place the tortellacci on top. Optional final move: chopped walnuts, pear slivers, or Parmigiano flakes – but even naked, they slay.

PUMPKIN & AMARETTI FAGOTTINI WITH SAGE BUTTER

A Renaissance banger from Mantua. Pumpkin, crushed amaretti, and Parmigiano wrapped in golden pasta, served with butter and fresh sage. Sweet, savory, iconic.

Ingredients

200 g roasted pumpkin, mashed (~¾ cup/7 oz)
30 g grated Parmigiano Reggiano (~¼ cup/1 oz)
10–15 g amaretti cookies, crumbled (~1 tbsp/0.5 oz)
grating of nutmeg, to taste
salt & pepper, to taste
200 g fresh egg pasta, shaped into fagottini (~1 ½ cups/7 oz)
    (see page 52)
100 g butter (~7.5 tbsp/3.5 oz)
6–8 fresh sage leaves
optional: Parmigiano Reggiano, to finish; crushed amaretti,
    for a crunchy twist

How to Make It

Prepare the filling. Use a dry, sweet pumpkin like Delica or Butternut. Roast it until soft and golden. Let it dry slightly (no one likes soggy fillings). Scoop it, mash it. Mix with Parmigiano, crushed amaretti, nutmeg, salt, and pepper. It should be sweet-salty-savory all in one mouthful. Chill it.

Roll out the pasta & shape the fagottini. As per the instructions on page 52. Cut into squares, dollop of filling in the center, fold diagonally, then pinch to make a pouch. Think: little parcels of emotional damage and fall flavors.

Cook the fagottini. Salted boiling water, for 4–5 minutes.

Make the sage butter. Melt butter in a pan, add sage leaves, let them crisp and infuse that nutty aroma. Take off the heat when golden, not burnt. (Burnt butter is not a vibe. Brown butter is.)

Drain pasta, toss in the sage butter, plate lovingly. Top with a dusting of Parmigiano and – if you're feeling cheeky – a sprinkle of amaretti crumble.

Bruna's Note

Pumpkin and amaretti? Sounds random, right? Wrong. Historical flex: this combo comes straight outta the Gonzaga court of Mantua, where the chefs weren't just making food – they were composing edible symphonies. Back in the 1500s, when pumpkins from the New World started popping up in Italy, those sugar-loving aristocrats thought, "Let's mix this veggie with cookies and see what happens." And spoiler: it slapped.

Add Parmigiano, nutmeg (which at the time cost more than gold), and BOOM, you've got a dish that tastes like baroque excess and holy indulgence. Still served today across Lombardy and Emilia-Romagna, especially during the holidays, because what says "Christmas spirit" better than buttery carbs and amaretti?

"

CACIO E PEPE CARAMELLE WITH BEURRE NOISETTE

Rome meets Paris and they make a pasta baby. Salty pecorino filling wrapped like candy, swimming in nutty brown butter that tastes like a plot twist.

Ingredients

100 g Pecorino Romano, finely grated (~2/3 cup/3.6 oz)
50 g Parmigiano Reggiano, finely grated (~6 tbsp/1.8 oz)
black pepper, cracked, to taste (but go hard or go home)
1 tbsp reserved pasta water or a few drops of cream, just to bind
optional: a teeny pinch of cornstarch to help with structure (0.5–1 g)
200 g fresh egg pasta, shaped into caramelle (~1 ½ cups/7 oz)
    (see page 52)
100 g butter (~7 tbsp/3.6 oz)
optional: fresh sage, for a herby accent; zest of ½ lemon,
    for brightness

How to Make It

Blend the grated cheeses with cracked black pepper. Add just enough pasta water or cream to make it pipeable or scoopable. Chill it a bit before filling. This is not a ricotta-based filling. This is pure cacio e pepe core: intense, dry, punchy.

Roll out the pasta & shape the caramelle. As per the instructions on page 52. Cut into rectangles, pipe a line of filling, roll up like a mini candy, pinch the ends. Visual vibes: pasta meets party favor.

Cook the caramelle in salty water. 4–5 minutes or until they float and look proud of themselves.

Make the beurre noisette like a true Frenchman. Melt butter in a light-colored pan (so you can see what's going on). Keep it on medium heat – swirl occasionally. You want the butter to foam, smell nutty, and turn golden brown, not black. Once it's amber and smells like roasted hazelnuts, pull it off the heat immediately. Optional: toss in a few sage leaves to crisp up, and/or lemon zest for balance.

Toss & serve. Drain the caramelle, toss gently in the brown butter. Plate with extra pepper, a dusting of cheese, and if you're feeling sexy, a drizzle of the browned bits from the bottom of the pan. That's where the flavor lives.

How NOT to ruin beurre noisette:
Don't walk away.
Don't check your phone.
Don't blink.
Brown butter goes from perfect to funeral pyre in like 4 seconds.
Use a light-colored pan, stay present, and when it's nutty and
golden, take it off the heat like it's a hot ex texting at 2am.

Traditional recipes – just not like your nonna made them

*Al Dente As F*ck*

CAPPELLI WITH RICOTTA, LEMON & ZUCCHINI BLOSSOMS

Bright, light, and garden-approved. A zesty ricotta filling wrapped in delicate pasta, topped with raw zucchini blossoms like edible confetti. Soft green flavors in their prettiest hat.

Ingredients

1 small zucchini, grated (~100 g/¾ cup /3.5 oz)
100 g ricotta (~½ cup/3.5 oz)
15 g Parmigiano Reggiano, grated (1 tbsp/0.5 oz)
zest of 1 lemon
salt & white pepper, to taste
optional: a few mint leaves, finely chopped
200 g fresh egg pasta, shaped into cappelli (~1 ½ cups/7 oz)
    (see page 51)
4–6 fresh zucchini blossoms, trimmed and torn by hand
1 tbsp olive oil (~15 ml/0.5 oz)
optional: a squeeze of lemon juice, a few extra raw zucchini
    shavings, super thin

How to Make It

Make the filling. Grate, salt, squeeze zucchini. Mix with ricotta, Parmigiano, lemon zest, salt, pepper, and mint if using. Keep it light and airy – this ain't a winter lasagna.

Roll out the pasta & shape the cappelli. As per the instructions on page 51. Cut rounds, place a dollop of filling, fold into "hats" – little chef's kisses made of dough.

Cook the cappelli. In salty boiling water for 4–5 minutes.

Plate like you're the goddess of summer. Toss the cooked cappelli gently in olive oil with a splash of lemon if you like. Plate them, and top with torn zucchini blossoms and maybe a few thin ribbons of raw zucchini.

Emanuele's Note

Don't cook the flowers. They're here for dramatic effect. Serve them raw, torn gently by hand (no knives please), and let them wilt just slightly from the warmth of the pasta. Want to feel fancy? Add a tiny drizzle of lemon oil or a grind of white pepper on top.

Traditional recipes – just not like your nonna made them

*Al Dente As F*ck*

CASUNZIEI ALL'AMPEZZANA

Alpine elegance in shocking pink. Beets, potatoes, brown butter, and poppy seeds, served hot, like an après-ski in edible form.

Ingredients

150 g cooked red beet (~⅔ cup/3.5 oz)
50 g boiled potato (~½ cup/3.5 oz)
20 g Parmigiano Reggiano, grated (~2 tbsp/0.7 oz)
salt & white pepper, to taste
optional: a pinch of nutmeg or a splash of melted butter
    for richness
200 g fresh egg pasta, shaped into casunziei (~1 ½ cups/7 oz)
    (see page 53)
100 g butter, melted and gently browned (~7 tbsp/3.6 oz)
1 tbsp poppy seeds (~10 g/0.35 oz)
optional: extra Parmigiano, grated; crushed black pepper,
    just a touch

How to Make It

Make the filling. Grate the cooked beet, mash the potato, mix with Parmigiano, salt, white pepper, optional nutmeg or butter. It should be creamy and vibrant – think Alpine hummus with a Master's degree.

Roll out the pasta & shape the casunziei. As per the instructions on page 51. Cut circles, place a small dollop of filling, fold into half-moons and press the edges tight. You want them delicate, not over-stuffed. Refined mountain elegance, not dumpling chaos.

Cook the pasta in salted water. For 4–5 minutes, until they float.

Butter & poppy party. Melt the butter, let it go just golden (or beurre noisette if you're feeling extra). Add poppy seeds, toast lightly, spoon generously over drained casunziei.

Bruna's Note
You can get fancy with sage or lemon zest, but honestly? Butter + poppy seeds = the whole point. It's the snowy Cortina ski lodge version of comfort food. Serve hot, breathe in deeply, and mentally wrap yourself in a wool blanket.

Traditional recipes – just not like your nonna made them

VINCISGRASSI

Lasagna's maximalist cousin from Marche. Technically, vincisgrassi should have 13 layers. But half is already delicious. Traditionally made with meat sauce and béchamel. And yes, that's spirulina in the dough. For dramatic effect, and a side of antioxidants.

Ingredients

½ onion, minced
½ carrot, minced
½ celery stalk, minced
2 tbsp olive oil
150 g ground pork (~1 cup/5.3 oz)
150 g ground beef mince (~1 cup/5.3 oz)
50 g chicken livers, chopped fine (¼ cup/1.8 oz)
1 small glass of dry white wine (~80 ml/⅓ cup)
1 tbsp tomato paste (~20 g/0.7 oz)
200 ml tomato passata (~¾ cup/7 oz)
salt & pepper to taste
optional: bay leaf or clove, for extra depth
30 g butter (2 tbsp/1.1 oz)
30 g flour (¼ cup/1.1 oz)
300 ml whole milk (1 ¼ cups/10 oz)
nutmeg, salt & white pepper to taste
200–250 g fresh egg pasta sheets (~1 ¾ cups / 8.8 oz)
        (see page 53)
optional green dough: add 5 g spirulina to the flour
50–70 g Parmigiano Reggiano, grated (~½ cup/2.5 oz)
butter for greasing the dish and dotting on top

How to Make It

Make the ragù. Sauté onion, carrot, celery in olive oil. For extra depth you can add a bay leaf or a clove. Add meats, brown well. Deglaze with wine. Stir in tomato paste, passata, salt, pepper. Simmer uncovered for 1–1.5 hours until thick and luscious.

Make the béchamel. Melt butter, add flour, cook 1–2 minutes. Slowly whisk in hot milk, stirring constantly until smooth. Season with nutmeg, salt, white pepper. Cook until just thickened.

Layer like a legend. No need to cook the pasta. The ragù juices will do the job. Trust us on this one. Grease a baking dish. Start layering: pasta › ragù › béchamel › Parmigiano. Repeat. Go for at least 7 layers, but 13 is the ultimate flex. Finish with a final layer of pasta, béchamel, Parmigiano, and a few dots of butter.

Bake until bubbly and golden. Preheated oven, 180°C/350°F for about 35–40 minutes.

Let it rest. Yes, seriously. 15–20 minutes. It needs to set so you don't serve lava soup.

Bruna's Note
This dish is a commitment. Like, *marriage-level* commitment. But it pays off in every creamy, meaty, cheesy bite. Bonus: it tastes even better the next day. If it survives the night.

MODERN RECIPES
— THINK ITALIAN
BUT JET-LAGGED

MALLOREDDUS WITH GARLIC, CASSAVA FAROFA & CARNE DE SOL

Italy meets Brazil in a crunchy, salty, smoky showdown. It's aglio e olio after two caipirinhas and a samba lesson.

Ingredients

2 tbsp olive oil (~30 ml/1 oz)
2 garlic cloves, thinly sliced
optional: chili flakes or fresh chili, to taste
1 tbsp butter or oil (~15 g/0.5 oz)
40 g cassava flour (big flakes, not powder!) (~⅓ cup/1.4 oz)
salt, to taste
optional: a pinch of smoked paprika or cumin
60 g carne de sol or beef jerky, shredded and toasted
 (~½ cup/2.1 oz)
300 g malloreddus (~1 ⅓ cups/7 oz dry pasta) (see page 48)
optional: chopped parsley, lime zest or a tiny squeeze of lime
 for brightness

How to Make It

Make the garlic oil. Sauté the garlic (and chili if using) in olive oil until golden and fragrant, not burned. Remove from heat, keep warm.

Toast the farofa. Melt butter in a pan, toss in cassava flour, stir constantly until golden and crispy. Season with salt and maybe paprika. This is your crunchy crown.

Crisp the carne de sol. In a hot pan, toast or fry the shredded meat until the edges are golden and it smells intense. You can lightly fry it in a dry pan until crisped, or in a splash of oil for extra indulgence.

Boil the malloreddus in salted water until al dente. Save some of the cooking water.

Assemble the dish. Toss drained malloreddus with garlic oil and a spoon or two of pasta water. Top with farofa, carne de sol, and optional herbs and lime.

Bruna's Note
I'm Brazilian, and this is my love letter to both countries. The chewy pasta, the garlic, the toasted farofa crunch, and that beef?

ORECCHIETTE WITH KIMCHI, CHARRED CORN & BLACK TRUFFLE

A Seoul-to-Puglia fever dream you didn't know you needed. This dish was born in Seoul, at 2am, slightly drunk and dangerously inspired. We just translated it into pasta language. The truffle isn't necessary, but it does scream "I've arrived".

Ingredients

1 corn cob or 100 g frozen corn, charred (~¾ cup/3.5 oz)
80 g kimchi, chopped (~⅔ cup/2.8 oz)
1 tbsp butter or oil (~15 g/0.5 oz)
300 g orecchiette (~1 ⅓ cups/7 oz dry pasta) (see page 49)
100 g mozzarella, torn (~¾ cup/3.5 oz)
a splash of pasta water
salt and pepper, to taste
black truffle, fresh or in flakes/shavings (~5–10 g/0.2–0.35 oz)
optional: extra mozzarella or grated Parm, if you're feeling it

How to Make It

Char the corn. If using a cob, grill it until it's got nice burnt bits, then slice off the kernels. If using frozen, toast the kernels in a dry pan until browned.

Grab the kimchi. Sauté the kimchi and corn in a bit of butter or oil for 2–3 minutes, until hot and vibey.

Boil the orecchiette in salted water until al dente. Save a splash of cooking water.

Mix it all. Toss the drained pasta with the kimchi + corn mixture. Add the mozzarella, let it melt slightly. Loosen with pasta water as needed. Season to taste.

Top with truffle. Optional, but let's be honest: encouraged. Serve warm and smug.

TROFIE WITH MAPO TOFU SAUCE

It's not fusion. It's full-on possession. Spicy, garlicky, crunchy, fermented, silky tofu on chewy pasta twists. This ain't a gentle embrace. This is a slap from both continents at once. If you serve this to your Italian aunt she might cry. And then ask for seconds.

Ingredients

120 g firm tofu, cut into cubes (~¾ cup/4.2 oz)
1 tsp neutral oil, to pan-fry
3 tbsp chili oil (~30 ml/1 oz)
6 garlic cloves, minced
2 spring onions, finely sliced (plus extra to top)
150 g ground pork or beef (~1 cup/5.3 oz)
1 ½ tbsp doubanjiang (fermented broad bean paste) (~22 g/0.75 oz)
1 ½ tbsp soy sauce (~22 ml/0.75 oz)
optional: 1 tsp Sichuan peppercorns, crushed
300 g trofie (~2 cups/10.6 oz dry pasta) (see page 50)
salt, to taste

How to Make It

Pan-fry the tofu in a nonstick pan with a bit of oil. Let it get golden and crispy on a few sides. Remove and set aside.

In the same pan, heat chili oil. Add garlic and spring onions. Sizzle until aromatic. Add the minced meat, sear hard until crispy and browned.

Add doubanjiang and soy sauce. Stir everything together to create a spicy, rich mess. Add tofu back in. Sprinkle in some crushed Sichuan pepper for the classic tingly drama.

Boil the trofie in salted water until al dente. Save some cooking water.

Toss the pasta with the Mapo tofu sauce. Add a splash of pasta water if needed to make the sauce cling to the pasta.

Top with fresh spring onion slices. Serve like the unapologetic legend you are.

PICI WITH MISO CREAM & LAO GAN MA

Creamy, spicy, oniony, and dangerously slurpable. This is the kind of pasta you eat directly from the pot with a big-ass fork and no shame. It's silky, spicy, and umami enough to qualify as emotional support food.

Ingredients

1 ½ tbsp butter or neutral oil (~30 g/1 oz)
2 spring onions, finely sliced (plus extra for topping),
    white bits separated
225 ml heavy cream (~1 cup/7.5 oz)
1 ½ tbsp white miso paste (~30 g/1 oz)
salt, but only if needed (miso is salty, so taste first)
3 tsp Lao Gan Ma (or your favorite crispy chili oil) (~15 g/0.5 oz)
300 g pici (~2 cups/10.6 oz) (see page 49)

How to Make It

Make the sauce. In a pan, melt butter and sauté the white bits of the spring onions until soft and a little golden.

Stir in cream and miso over low heat. Let it melt together slowly – no boiling. Add a splash of pasta water if it feels too thick. Taste and add more salt, if needed.

Add Lao Gan Ma right at the end. Just enough to heat through and swirl that chili magic into the mix.

Boil the pici in salted water. Don't rush them – thick noodles take their time. Save some pasta water.

Toss the pici straight into the sauce. Mix until glossy and glorious.

Top with spring onion greens. And, if you're wild, another spoon of chili oil.

FREGULA SARDA WITH CHILI-STYLE TOPPING & SOUR CREAM

Italy, meet Texas. You're gonna get along just fine. This is a one-way ticket from Sardinia to San Antonio. Fregula holds up like a champ.

Ingredients

300 g fregula sarda pasta (~1 ¾ cup/10.6 oz) (see page 48)
900 ml beef stock (~4 cups/34 oz)
1 garlic clove, minced
1–2 fresh hot peppers, chopped (your choice!)
1 tbsp olive oil (~15 ml/0.5 oz)
200 g ground beef (~1 ⅓ cups/7 oz)
100 g tomato pulp or passata (~⅓ cup/3.5 oz)
80 g canned red kidney beans, rinsed (~½ cup/2.8 oz)
80 g canned black beans, rinsed (~½ cup/2.8 oz)
1 tsp chili powder
salt and pepper, to taste
1 jalapeño, sliced
2 tbsp sour cream (~30 g/1 oz), dotted on top
zest of ½ lime
optional: chopped green herbs and/or red onion rings, to top

How to Make It

Cook the fregula in simmering beef stock. Until just tender but still with a bite (10–12 minutes). Drain if needed, then set aside in a shallow bowl.

Make the chili topping. In a hot pan, sauté garlic and peppers in olive oil. Add ground beef and sear until crispy. Toss in the tomato pulp, beans, chili powder, salt, and pepper. Simmer for 5–10 minutes until thick and sexy.

Assemble. Spoon the fregula into bowls like a cozy grain base. Gently ladle the chili mixture on top – don't mix it in or you'll end up with sad baby food.

Top it all. Dot with sour cream, slices of jalapeño, grate over some lime zest, and hit it with herbs and red onion rings if you've got 'em.

Bruna's Note
Small but firm note on herbs: you can top this with parsley, chives, spring onion – hell, even microgreens if you're feeling dramatic. But if you reach for cilantro... I will judge you. I will delete your number. I will pretend we never shared this recipe.
It's not personal. It's just that cilantro tastes like betrayal and soap. Pick another leaf.

TAGLIOLINI "NOODLES" IN MUSHROOM BROTH

A quiet storm of umami, veggies, and silky pasta with an identity crisis. This dish is calm, but powerful. Like a mushroom monk whispering secrets into your mouth. And if you burn the spring onion on purpose? Even better. Char is flavor. Zen is chaos. Pasta is life.

Ingredients

650 ml water (~2 ½ cups/22 oz)
20 g dried shiitake mushrooms (~1 cup when rehydrated/0.7 oz)
1 small piece of kombu (dried kelp) (~5 g/0.2 oz)
1 tbsp soy sauce (~15 ml/0.5 oz)
1 tsp mirin or rice vinegar (~5 ml/0.17 oz)
optional: a splash of mushroom or veggie bouillon for deeper flavor
50 g fresh shiitake, sliced (~½ cup/1.8 oz)
50 g champignon mushrooms, sliced (~½ cup/1.8 oz)
50 g beech mushrooms, trimmed (~½ cup/1.8 oz)
1 tbsp toasted sesame oil (~15 ml/0.5 oz)
salt, to taste
2 baby bok choy, halved
200 g tagliolini (~1 ½ cups/7 oz) (see page 55)
1 tbsp sesame seeds, white or black (~10 g/0.35 oz)
1 spring onion, raw or lightly charred
optional: soft-boiled egg, shredded chicken, or pork belly
    (not today though – ours is veg)

How to Make It

Make the broth. In a pot, combine water, dried shiitake, and kombu. Simmer gently for 20–25 minutes. Remove solids, then add soy sauce and mirin. Taste and reduce slightly if it needs punch. Set aside, keep hot.

Cook the mushrooms. In a pan, sauté all fresh mushrooms in a splash of sesame oil until golden and a bit caramelized. Salt lightly.

Blanch the bok choy. Literally 30–60 seconds in boiling water, just enough to soften the whites and keep the greens perky. Drain and set aside.

Boil the tagliolini until just tender. Drain, rinse very briefly under hot water if needed to keep them loose.

Assemble like a minimalist. Put noodles in bowls, pour over hot mushroom broth, arrange bok choy and mushrooms like you're styling a spa menu. Drizzle with sesame oil, add sesame seeds, top with spring onion (raw or lightly charred).

Optional protein? Add gently on top. But honestly, it's perfect as is.

TAGLIATELLE WITH CREAMY CAJUN SHRIMP SAUCE

Mais yeah, ma chérie, this pasta got more kick than a swamp gator. A little Italy, a little Louisiana, a whole lotta YES.

Ingredients

300 g tagliatelle (~2 ¼ cups/11.6 oz) (see page 55)
    For the marinade:
330 g pink shrimp, deveined but not peeled (~2 ¼ cups/11.6 oz)
1 garlic clove, minced
½ fresh chili, finely sliced
1 tbsp chopped parsley (~5 g/0.17 oz)
1 tsp lemon juice (~5 ml/0.17 oz)
1 tbsp olive oil or butter (~15 g/0.5 oz)
1 tbsp Cajun seasoning (~10 g/0.35 oz) – homemade
    or store-bought
    For the sauce:
2 garlic cloves, minced
300 ml heavy cream (~1 ½ cup/10.2 oz)
optional: 1 tsp smoked paprika
50 g grated Parmigiano Reggiano (~½ cup/1.8 oz)
cracked black pepper, to taste
optional: a squeeze of lemon to finish

How to Make It

Make the shrimp marinade. Combine garlic, fresh chili, chopped parsley, and lemon juice. Toss the shrimp in the marinade, and let them sit for 10–15 minutes while you prep the sauce.

Cook the shrimp. Sear the marinated shrimp in olive oil or butter with half the Cajun seasoning until pink and slightly browned. Remove and set aside.

In the same pan, toss in garlic. Let it sizzle 30 seconds, then pour in cream. Add smoked paprika, remaining Cajun seasoning, and Parm. Let it thicken slightly over low heat.

Toss the shrimp back into the sauce. Stir and simmer just enough to heat through.

Cook the pasta in salted water until al dente. Save a splash of the cooking water.

Toss the tagliatelle in the sauce. Add a splash of pasta water if it needs loosening. Stir like you mean it.

Finish with a flourish. Add cracked black pepper on top and a squeeze of lemon if you're feeling zesty.

Emanuele's Note
Don't rely on sad store-bought blends – make your own Cajun seasoning and feel the power. You'll need: 1 tsp paprika (sweet or smoked), ½ tsp garlic powder, ½ tsp onion powder, ½ tsp dried oregano, ½ tsp dried thyme, ¼ tsp cayenne pepper (more if you like pain), ½ tsp black pepper, ½ tsp salt. Mix everything together and store in a jar.

Modern recipes – think italian but jet-lagged

PAPPARDELLE WITH KORESH BADEMJAN & BARBERRIES

Persian soul. Italian carbs. Zero compromises. Well, a few compromises in Emanuele's note on the bottom of this page, but zero compromises on flavor.

Ingredients

1 medium eggplant (~250 g/9 oz)
250 g lamb shoulder, cubed (~1 ½ cups/8.8 oz)
olive oil, for frying
1 small onion, finely chopped
1 garlic clove, minced
2 tbsp tomato paste (~30 g/1 oz)
½ tsp turmeric
pinch of saffron threads, bloomed in 2 tbsp hot water
400 ml lamb/veg broth (~1 ⅔ cups/13.5 oz)
salt and black pepper, to taste
optional: 50 g semi-dried tomatoes, chopped (~½ cup/1.8 oz)
300 g pappardelle (~2 ¼ cups/11.6 oz) (see page 54)
30 g dried barberries (zereshk) (~3 tbsp/1 oz)
1 tbsp butter or oil (~15 g/0.5 oz)
1 tsp sugar

How to Make It

Prep the eggplant. Peel in alternating strips – so it crisps beautifully but still soaks up the sauce. Pan-fry or roast until golden-soft. Set aside.

Brown the lamb in oil until caramelized. Add onion and garlic; sauté until translucent.

Add tomato paste, turmeric, and bloomed saffron. Cook for 2 minutes, then add broth. Season and simmer gently for 45–60 minutes until lamb is fall-apart tender.

Add the eggplant. Fold in the cooked eggplant (and optional semi-dried tomatoes) in the last 15 minutes of cooking.

Cook the pappardelle to al dente. Drain and gently toss with the sauce.

Prepare barberries. Soak briefly, then pan-fry with butter and sugar until shiny and tangy.

Top each bowl with the barberry jewel crown. Don't stir, this is *presentation meets flavor shock.*

Emanuele's Note

Koresh hacks, or how to not offend anyone but still cheat a little:

- Lazy day? You can slow-cook the meat in advance and just reduce the sauce when ready to serve.
- Saffron budget tight? The saffron is a non-negotiable gold touch. Use less, but bloom it properly in hot water. That golden magic goes a long way.
- Going veggie? Sub the lamb with seared mushrooms (portobello or king oyster) and boost umami with a splash of soy sauce or miso.
- No barberries? Dried cranberries soaked in lemon water work in a pinch. But you didn't hear it from us.

Modern recipes – think italian but jet-lagged

LASAGNA AL VOL-AU-VENT

When Belgian comfort food sneaks into your nonna's sacred Sunday dish. Parm + Gouda is diplomacy. Meatballs are your hype crew. And yes, you can call it "Lasagn-au-Vent." We won't stop you.

Ingredients

For the mini meatballs:

1 slice of white bread, crust removed
40 ml milk (~2 ½ tbsp/1.35 oz)
250 g ground veal or chicken (~1 ¼ cups/8.8 oz)
1 small egg
30 g grated Parmigiano Reggiano (~¼ cup/1 oz)
1 garlic clove, grated

For the velouté:

40 g butter (3 tbsp/1.4 oz)
40 g flour (⅓ cup/ 1.4 oz)
400 ml chicken stock (1 ⅔ cups / 13.5 oz)
salt, pepper, and nutmeg, to taste

6–8 fresh lasagna sheets (~180–200 g/6.3–7 oz) (see page 54)
150 g cooked guinea fowl (you can sub this with chicken, no one will get offended), shredded (~1 cup/5.3 oz)
250 g champignons de Paris, cleaned and cooked
50 g grated Parmigiano Reggiano (~½ cup/1.8 oz)
50 g grated aged Gouda (~½ cup/1.8 oz)
optional: splash of chicken broth to loosen the mix

How to Make It

Make the mini meatballs. Soak bread in milk, then squeeze out excess. Mix ground meat, egg, Parm, and garlic. Season with salt and pepper. Be careful not to overwork the mix. Roll into marble-sized balls (~2 cm/¾ inch). Pan-fry for 5–6 minutes until browned and cooked. Set aside.

Make the velouté. Melt butter, add flour, cook for 1–2 minutes. Slowly whisk in chicken stock, stirring constantly until smooth. Season with nutmeg, salt, and white pepper. Cook until just thickened.

Assemble the lasagna. Preheat oven to 180°C/350°F. No need to blanch your pasta sheets. Mix guinea fowl and champignons de Paris with velouté and two cheeses. Layer as follows:
- bottom of tray: a spoon of velouté
- pasta sheet
- filling mix + scattered mini meatballs
- repeat until the top
- final layer = pasta + velouté + optional dusting of cheese

Bake until bubbling. Cook for 25-30 minutes, optionally broil for 2–3 minutes for golden top.

SORPRESINE IN TOM KHA KAI

Your Italian priest just booked a one-way ticket to Bangkok. Yes, there's cilantro in here. No, I don't like it. Yes, it makes sense.

Ingredients

400 ml coconut milk (~1⅔ cups/13.5 oz)
200 ml chicken stock (~¾ cup/6.7 oz)
1 stalk lemongrass, bruised and cut in chunks
2 cm fresh galangal, sliced (or ginger, if desperate)
3 kaffir lime leaves, torn
2 Thai bird's eye chilies, smashed
100 g mushrooms, sliced (~1 cup/3.5 oz)
150 g chicken thighs, thinly sliced (~1 cup/5.3 oz)
1 tbsp fish sauce (~15 ml/0.5 oz)
2 limes, 1 juiced and 1 cut in wedges
salt, to taste
180 g fresh sorpresine pasta (~1⅓ cups/6.3 oz) (see page 56)
optional (but traditional): fresh cilantro (I know, I know what I said
1 spring onion, thinly sliced
optional: extra chili oil if you like pain

How to Make It

In a pot, combine the coconut milk and stock. Add lemongrass, galangal, lime leaves, and chilies. Simmer for 10 minutes to get that aromatic punch.

Strain out the chunks if you don't want a mouthful of stalks. Up to you.

Add mushrooms and sliced chicken. Simmer for 5–7 minutes until chicken is cooked. Don't let it boil too hard or it'll split.

Season with fish sauce, lime juice, and salt. Taste it. It should be sour, salty, spicy, creamy. You'll know.

Cook the sorpresine in salted water until al dente. Drain gently.

Serve the broth hot. Pour over the pasta, top with optional cilantro (*sigh*), lime, spring onion, and chili oil.

al dente
as fuck

FARFALLE WITH MUSSELS, GUANCIALE & SALTY HERBS

Straight from the shores of Zeeland to your Roman arteries. We live in Zeeland. Mussels are practically our neighbors. But guanciale? That's bloodline stuff. This dish doesn't pick sides, it unites.

Ingredients

2 tbsp olive oil (~30 ml/1 oz)
1 garlic clove, crushed
½ small shallot, finely chopped
500 g fresh mussels, cleaned (~1.1 lbs/~4 cups in shell)
40 ml dry white wine (~3 tbsp/1.3 oz)
130 g guanciale, cut into lardons (~1 cup/4.6 oz)
300 g farfalle (~2 ¼ cups/10.6 oz) (see page 53)
salty herbs mix, chopped: fresh thyme, samphire,
    and sea fennel or parsley
black pepper, to taste
optional: zest of ½ lemon for zing

How to Make It

Add olive oil, garlic, and shallot to a hot pot. Sauté until fragrant.

Toss in mussels and wine. Cover and steam for 2–3 minutes until mussels open. Discard any that don't. Strain and reserve the cooking liquid. Remove most mussels from shells (keep a few in-shell to finish).

In a pan, crisp the guanciale until golden and glorious. No oil needed, it brings its own fat party.

Deglaze with a bit of the mussel broth. Let it reduce slightly, then add the shelled mussels and a splash more of their broth.

Boil farfalle in salted water until al dente. Save some pasta water. Toss into the sauce with herbs, a grind of pepper, and optional lemon zest. Mix gently.

Plate. Serve with shell-on mussels on top, a drizzle of oil, and more herbs.

Bruna's Note

For our Northern Hemisphere folk: only eat mussels in months with an R? Not just folklore, it's coastal logic. Colder months = fatter, juicier, cleaner mollusks. Summer ones? Meh. They're tired, skinny, and mid-spawning. In Zeeland, we start in July, but the real juicy ones hit in September. Be patient. Let them bulk.

Modern recipes – think italian but jet-lagged